Beyond the Veil

The no-nonsense guide to spiritual & psychic development

Lucy Baker

Contents

Acknowledgments

It would be impossible to mention everyone who has positively impacted on my journey up to this point by name. However, there are some people who simply cannot go without mention. Firstly, I would like to thank my editors, Lisa Annunziato and Cristina Swink. Without their help, this book would most likely have been nothing more than an impressive demonstration of spelling errors and word vomit. I am eternally grateful for your expertise.

Thank you to my parents and my sisters, who have supported me unconditionally, throughout the darkest of times, and who never gave up on me even when they wanted to throttle me.

BEYOND THE VEIL

To my husband, the non-believer and master of the eye roll…. I love you with all of my heart. Thank you for putting up with me…. you're a trooper!

To my children, Jacob, Mimi, Dylan, and Harry: You make me proud every single day and are the four greatest things that I have achieved in this lifetime. You are my world. Ps…. please tidy your bedrooms.

Jen, I don't thank you enough for your unwavering support. Your capacity to remain level-headed during times of spiritual f**kery is unrivaled and I appreciate you always.

To each and every one of my students, friends, and tribe, who keep me sane and remind me daily of how beautiful people can truly be. I love you all.

And lastly but by no means least…. to Claire Sage. There are simply no words to adequately convey the gratitude that I have for having met you accidentally, during what seems like an entire lifetime ago. I have absolutely no doubt that without your support, guidance, and friendship I would still be rocking in a corner fully believing that I was losing my mind. You were my savior and I will treasure your friendship always.

BEYOND THE VEIL

"The rabbit hole went straight on like a tunnel for some way, and then dipped suddenly down, so suddenly that Alice had not a moment to think about stopping herself before she found herself falling down what seemed to be a very deep well."

Alice's Adventures in Wonderland,
by Lewis Carroll

BEYOND THE VEIL

Introduction

In no way was this book ever intended to be autobiographical, but as the only logical place to start is at the beginning, I must first explain how these experiences came into existence in my life. This is a story in and of itself.

I never considered for even one second that I was gifted. Thinking back to my early childhood, I had an invisible friend called Adam, who I remember playing with in my bedroom. At the time I believed Adam to be an 'imaginary friend' but with hindsight, it is clear to me that he wasn't imaginary at all and that I was actually playing with the spirit of a young boy. I had completely forgotten all about him until very recently when the discovery of my childhood 'care-bear' in the loft brought back a vivid memory of an incident that happened when I was around six years of age. On this particular night, I was woken up in the early hours of the morning. The house was quiet, and I knew immediately that my parents had already gone to bed. My bedroom door was ajar, and I knew that there was a man standing on the landing outside my bedroom door. I couldn't see him, but I could feel his presence strongly, and even at the age of six, I knew for sure that his intentions toward my family and me were not good. I was quite convinced that he was an intruder who planned to hurt us. With what seemed like a very rational solution to me at the time, I offered him my beloved care-bear and said he could keep it if he didn't hurt us. I remember lying in bed with the covers pulled up to my chin and closing my eyes tightly praying that he would leave. I also remember being quite shocked and incredibly relieved when eventually I opened my eyes, sensing that he was gone, and discovered my care-bear still sitting at the end of my bed! Looking back, I believe that night resulted in me partially blocking my gifts through fear.

My gifts didn't completely disappear, I just had no idea whatsoever that they were gifts at all. The many nights I spent lying in bed with the covers pulled up to my chin because I was frightened were attributed to an overactive imagination. I would frequently be unable to get to sleep, convinced that I could see dark figures in my room, standing in a corner or at the end of my bed. Then morning would come, and I'd curse myself for keeping myself awake imagining monsters in my room. I remember one particular family holiday in Umbria, Italy when I was 17. My parents had rented an absolutely stunning villa that had a stone outbuilding separate to the main house. To the side of the building was a door that opened to a staircase leading to the most amazing bedroom. With thick stone walls and solid wooden beams, it was an absolutely stunning room and looked like something out of a fairytale. Being the eldest daughter (and keen to have an excuse to leave the main building so I could smoke cigarettes without my parents knowing), I picked that room as my own for the week. The minute I went up those stairs to sleep on the first night of our stay I knew straight away what a terrible choice I had made! I don't think I slept for more than two hours a night during the entire week. The moment I would reach the top of the staircase that led into the bedroom I could feel a presence watching me. At night time I would turn on all of the lights and climb into the bed. I was too scared to lie down as that made me feel even more vulnerable, so I would sit up in the

13

bed with my back pressed up against the headboard and the sheets pulled up to my chin. I would sense a woman frantically pacing at the end of the bed never taking her eyes off me. In my mind's eye, I could see her clearly, with her long mousy brown hair falling over the shoulders of her white nightgown. I was terrified to close my eyes, certain that if I did, I would later open them to see her right up in my face screaming. In the early hour's exhaustion would start to set in, and still afraid to lie down, I would sleep sitting upright, covers held up around my ears and with only the sound of the mosquitos who had been drawn to the lights for company.

Despite constantly being unsettled at night I always had somewhat of an obsession with horror movies. Of course, I would be utterly terrified after they finished but I couldn't help but watch them. Looking back, it was as though I was constantly seeking knowledge on what I knew deep down was real. On one particular occasion, the movie *The Exorcist* was re-released at our local cinema. Stupidly I agreed that going to the midnight showing of the movie was a brilliant idea. When I returned home at 2am I was so scared to go to sleep that I woke my 11yr old sister up at 2:30am and told her she had to come and sleep in my bed with me because I was afraid to sleep on my own. This was a terrible plan, as I discovered at 4am when I awoke to find a girl looking very much like the subject of the movie right in my face. It had not occurred to me when I woke my sister and dragged her into my bed that at the age of eleven, with her long dark hair, she bore such a striking resemblance to the central character of the film! The poor child was evicted from my bed immediately!

I hated being alone at night and would always sleep with the lights on when I could. I also couldn't stand to be without noise. I would inevitably have the television on in the background. Silence always made me feel on edge. Crowds of people were also a big issue for me. Busy shops, elevators with strangers inside, and meeting groups of people often felt like torture. With hindsight, I can now see that being an empath was affecting me greatly; however, not even knowing what an empath was for most of my life, I always put it down to being socially inept and awkward. For those not familiar with this term, empaths are people who have the psychic ability to discern and often take on the mental and emotional state of others. I never really understood why I didn't 'fit in', and always knew deep down that there was something missing.

I grew up, got married, settled down, and had my four beautiful children. On paper, I had everything I had ever wanted, but for many years I knew I was looking for something. I just had absolutely no idea what it was, so I would flit from one thing to the next, constantly searching for the piece of the puzzle that was eluding me.

In 2010 we moved into our current home in Leicestershire, England and for the first few years that we lived here, I was always aware of a presence. The wardrobe door would open a fraction and close, or a light would flicker, and I would say, *"Hello Elizabeth"*. Those of you who have raised children yourselves will be acutely aware that during their preschool years much time is spent multi-tasking or on autopilot not really paying much attention to anything other than the constant mayhem of trying to get through the never-ending list of chores. It was only when one of the children asked me why I called *"our ghost"* Elizabeth, that it dawned on me that I had just woken up one morning knowing her name. I didn't notice that moment that Elizabeth left us, but once I realized she was gone I missed her. She had been rather a lovely presence in our home.

Alfred was another matter entirely. He was with us

for almost a month. I would see him staring at me around doorways and feel his eyes on me constantly. He made me feel hideously uncomfortable whenever I was alone in the house. My husband teased me over and over again for winding myself up with all this 'nonsense' and blamed my overactive imagination whilst laughing at me for getting myself so worked up over something that wasn't even real. He asked, "Why do you call him Alfred?" Again, I realized that I just woke up one day and knew his name. Then one evening we were standing in the hallway and I mentioned Alfred. All of a sudden, Molly our springer spaniel started barking like crazy at the wall. Even as the world's biggest skeptic my husband couldn't discount how strange an occurrence that was, especially given that Molly wasn't a dog that was ever known to bark. About a week later, much to my relief, Alfred disappeared as suddenly as he had arrived.

Still, despite all of this, not once did I ever consider that I had gifts or was a medium. That sort of stuff was crazy talk. I was just a stay at home mum of 4 who every now and again had experienced a 'ghostly encounter'.

Then began my Dark Night of the Soul. This term

comes from a 16th century Catholic mystic & priest, St. John of the Cross, that refers to a collapse of one's sense of meaning in life, leaving nothing to make sense. At the time, of course, I had no idea that this was what I was experiencing but it touched the very foundations of my soul. In 2012, following a personal tragedy, when my husband and I lost a daughter, I fell into a deep depression that I managed to hide for far longer than I should have. With my depression came acute anxiety and guilt and I fell into a big black hole of despair. I was angry all the time and felt completely lost. My self-esteem was long gone, and I was a complete and utter mess.

It was at this time that I began experiencing the horrific phenomenon of sleep paralysis. I remember my first episode like it was yesterday. I woke up from sleep and could see a huge black mass of smoke next to my bed. I felt myself being dragged from my bed by my hair and no matter how much I tried to fight, move or scream I was helpless. That night I was far too afraid to even attempt to go back to sleep, so I went downstairs and found myself trying to find any explanation for what I had just experienced. I was rather embarrassed and a little horrified to be searching 'demonic possessions' online, but at the time it was the only thing I could think to search for information on. Of course, I found nothing of any use to me, until I finally stumbled across a vague description of sleep paralysis. I discovered that sleep paralysis is a sleep disorder that leaves a person temporarily paralyzed during awakening or falling asleep. It very often triggers a fear response leading to panic and hallucinations.

As much as I was reassured to have some sort of medical explanation for this horrific and terrifying experience, and as hard as I tried to convince myself that maybe this could explain away all the previous experiences of the shadows I had always seen in my room, it did nothing to alleviate my fear. I soon realized that during all of my other experiences of seeing shadows and being afraid prior to this, I wasn't paralyzed, nor was I awakening or falling asleep, so despite trying I could not explain it away. For the next few years, triggered by my growing anxiety, sleep paralysis pretty much ruled my life. Bedtime became a dirty word, and I would stay up until the early hours trying to ensure that I was so tired when I went to bed that I would fall into a deep sleep and not have time to be afraid. It didn't help. The episodes became more and more frequent and eventually were occurring almost nightly. I would awaken to feel myself being dragged from my bed by my feet, would see swirling black masses clambering up from the bottom of the bed or find myself being pinned down by dark shadows sitting on my chest suffocating me. Try as I might, I couldn't move, I couldn't scream, and I was totally unable to do anything to stop it. I would eventually awaken fully, terrified, sweating, heart pounding and often in tears. I'd either grab hold of my sleeping husband and cling to him for dear life or make a break for it and move to the sofa. Sleeping on the sofa with the lights and the television on was 'safe'. I was in a constant state of terror once I got into bed and took to drinking until 3 or 4am each morning hoping that if I passed out, I could escape the episodes. In no time at all, between the depression, the anxiety, and the sleep issues, I found myself looking in the mirror to see an alcoholic in a permanent state of exhaustion staring back at me.

On one particular morning, I remember sitting up in bed at 8am on the phonc to my doctor. I was practically delirious from exhaustion, and he couldn't understand a word I said down the phone between sobs as I pleaded for anything that would help me sleep. I would have willingly handed my soul to the devil himself at that point for a full 8 hours of sleep! Even now, with all of the knowledge I have absorbed and had to learn over the last few years, I still believe that to be something I would have genuinely considered. There is nothing on this earth that can cause a person to unravel as quickly and as dramatically as exhaustion. I wasn't just tired. I was utterly sleep deprived, trying desperately to function when I was only getting a few hours of poor-quality sleep at night and I was completely losing the ability and the desire to function, mentally, physically, and emotionally. Before long I hit the inevitable rock bottom. I was diagnosed with acute anxiety disorder and depression and began the rocky road to recovery. I was given sleeping pills to aid my constant exhaustion, and as my anxiety was brought more under control, I realized that the only thing that was truly going to turn my situation around was to stop drinking too. If I didn't, I was never going to get out of the big black hole I had been in for so long.

Despite the medication and my newfound sobriety, I felt unbalanced and 'wobbly' all the time. The only thing I could think might help was yoga so in desperation I gave it a shot. I didn't help. I am not even remotely bendy, but what did help was the breathing. So, meditation became my crutch. I tried to meditate every day, even if it was only for a few minutes, and within a few months, I was beginning to feel that I was gaining some control back. I was finding a new sense of calm. Within twelve months I was able to manage what remained of my anxiety with meditation alone and was able to come off my medication entirely. I began sleeping properly for the first time in years and started to feel like me again. The only problem was that I still had no idea who that 'me' really was.

I was now meditating regularly, and my confidence and trust in myself was slowly returning. I began feeling drawn to crystals and had started a small collection of crystal pendants that I would swap around and wear daily depending on what I felt was right for me at the time. I started growing lavender for its calming and relaxing properties and burning essential oils daily to help me stay calm and relaxed. What I didn't realize at the time was that I was finally following my intuition. I instinctively knew what I needed to help myself heal, and I had managed to quiet my mind enough to actually listen.

One evening I suddenly felt compelled to start learning about Wicca. When questioned about religion in the past, my response had always been the same. "I believe in something. I just don't know what that something is!". So far, following my intuition was working out pretty well, so I dutifully downloaded a few books onto my kindle and started reading. A lot of it made sense to me. It wasn't a 'perfect' fit, but herbs, oils, and crystals had already become a part of my daily life so what harm could it do to learn more? Within a matter of days, I was bored. This was all obvious stuff that I already knew. I didn't want to learn by just reading. I had questions and I wanted to be able to interact and learn from actual people rather than just words on a page. So, I logged into my Facebook account wondering if there might be any groups that may be of help. I joined a few of these groups, made a couple of posts, asked some questions and enjoyed learning from them. But never in my wildest imagination did I consider for even a moment, just how important this little dalliance would prove to be in my spiritual journey!

On the night of my spiritual awakening, I went to bed as usual. Sleep paralysis had not been an issue for me for many months, and whilst I would still often feel some presence in my room and see shadows in the corners I would try to meditate in bed whilst I went to sleep to curb any anxiety that could trigger an episode.

There truly is no way that I can explain what happened on this night without minimizing how truly terrifying it really was. I am not sure the right words even exist, but I will relay what happened as accurately as I can.

I woke up in the dark to see an old woman in a black hooded cloak kneeling on my bed between my husband and me. The room was almost pitch black but the small slant of light coming from the gap in the blind seemed to illuminate her from behind. She was looking down over me, almost looming, but at first, I didn't feel threatened exactly, more apprehensive, as I lay there waiting to see what was going to happen. I was already quite sure that this was not sleep paralysis. I had already turned my head to stare straight at her. Then suddenly, without any warning she lurched forwards with her arms outstretched and with her pale bony hands she began grabbing right in front of my face. I could see and feel a black fog all around me and as she grabbed at it with her hand, she was continuously dragging it upwards, across my chest and up over my face. I felt like I was choking. The black fog was oppressive and heavy and as it was pulled up over my mouth I struggled to breathe and began to panic. After what seemed like forever she stopped and just stared at me. By this point I was petrified. I opened my mouth and I screamed. I screamed, and I screamed, and I screamed! I awoke suddenly and sat bolt upright in bed shaking and sweating and promptly burst into tears. My husband was sat up, wide awake just staring at me. "What the hell just happened?" he asked. He then explained to me that I had been screaming so hysterically that despite his attempts to wake me up he had not been able to do so until in desperation he had panicked and punched me in the chest which is what had finally woken me from my sleep. The next day, still visibly shaken he turned to me and said, "I've never heard anything like that before. I always thought the phrase 'blood curdling' scream was nonsense until I heard your screams last night!".

Still scared and very shaken up, I needed answers. What the hell had just happened to me? This was not sleep paralysis, and I was just as sure that this was no ordinary nightmare! It was too real. I had felt it, I had lived this experience and for the first time in my life, I knew with absolute certainty that this was not my imagination. Even my infallible skeptic of a husband was shaken up. So, I reached out to the only people I could think of who I felt sure wouldn't laugh in my face and tell me I was crazy. I posted a description of my experience in a witchcraft group and pleaded for answers. Only one person responded with an interpretation that made any sense to me at all. This person wrote that it sounded very much like the veil had been lifted from me. The black fog being described as a veil rang true to me immediately, so I made a mental note of her name knowing instinctively that this person was someone I could trust to help me figure things out if anything like this ever happened again. Little did I know at the time that this person would become not only my mentor but one of my dearest friends. I had just met Claire Sage.

Far too terrified to even consider sleeping in my bed, I decided to camp out on the sofa for a few nights with the lights on and watch movies in the hope that I would eventually fall to sleep. Halfway through the first film I caught myself unable to keep looking over to the opposite corner of the room. I could feel the presence of a woman and a young boy there, and no matter how much I tried to tell myself that I was imagining it, or how many times I rubbed my eyes, I realized that I could not only sense them, but I could also see. I could see waves of energy flickering and shifting, almost like a haze, in the form of an elderly woman. I took a photograph on my phone and started studying it. Sure enough, I could make out the old lady in the photograph. The only thing I could think to do was to send a message to Claire Sage. I wasn't sure if she would even read it as she had no idea who

I was, let alone actually respond to me, but I sent it anyway, along with the photograph I had taken. Much to my relief Claire reassured me that I was not crazy, and that as a medium, she could also clearly see the spirits in my living room. So, until the early hours of the following morning, I sat on the sofa, with one eye on the tv and the other of the corner of the room. I didn't feel afraid, more bemused with a hundred questions flying around in my head, reassuring myself that Claire said I wasn't crazy.

After a few more nights of bewildered observations of spirits in my living room, I felt brave enough to venture back upstairs to try sleeping in my own bed in the dark. After some time spent trying to drift off, I became aware of something moving up and down at the end of the bed. Even in the pitch dark I could see the little dark-haired boy pushing a toy car back and forth along the footboard of the bed. He was wearing a stripy vest and shorts and totally engrossed in playing by himself. Back to the sofa and the security of the downstairs lights I went!

I trawled Facebook for psychic groups desperate for some sort of reasonable explanation for what I was seeing and experiencing, and when I finally found one that seemed relevant, I requested to join it. I had no idea at the time that one of the moderators of this group was Claire Sage! Sleep was out of the question over the following weeks, so I decided to make use of my nights by learning everything I could. I discovered that not only could I see spirits in my own home, but I could also see them in other people's photos in the psychic groups too. So, I started reading other people's photos, always pushing myself to step out of my comfort zone. Claire had the patience of a saint with my constant questions and need for validation on the things I was seeing, and as I started to need less validation and trust what I was picking up, she started to teach me how to work with the gift I had been given. She told me about her own spirit guide and I was able to connect with one of my guides, Willow, which also helped me enormously. The few nights I had planned to spend on the sofa had turned into seven long weeks. But in that time, something pretty magical had happened. Without me even realizing it, I had stopped feeling afraid and had started to embrace my gifts.

September had arrived, the new school year was about to begin and I knew that I would never manage to get all four children to school on time existing on too few snatched hours of sleep on the sofa, so it was time for me to head back upstairs to sleep in the dark, on the condition that I could install a small night light in our room. It was one thing managing not to freak out when I knew something was there and the lights were on, but that dark bedroom had also been the location of some of my most terrifying experiences, so if I was going to make it back to my own room, I needed a light on so that I felt 'safe'.

Now that I had finally braved the dark and quiet of my bedroom, I started getting nightly visions from earthbound spirits who had not yet crossed over. In a strange way, these actually made it easier for me to get to sleep. If I stayed relaxed, I got to watch mini movie trailers in my head and try to piece together everything I was being shown. From time to time I would be shown something upsetting or disturbing, but I was able to quickly shut it down if I ever felt uncomfortable or something I was shown made me jump. I vividly remember lying in bed one night and thinking to myself "Ha! I'm finally getting the hang of this!". I spoke too soon. Far too soon!

I continued to read in groups and worked on developing my gifts daily, and initially, I attributed the rapid increase of spirit activity in my home to my higher vibrations and greater awareness of what was going on around me. I found myself constantly distracted by the astonishing levels of activity in my home. My husband and I would sit down to relax and watch something on the television after putting the children to bed, and I would constantly have my attention drawn elsewhere and sit watching the spirits present in the room instead. I often wondered how on earth it was even possible that I had never noticed them all before. The amount of spirit energy in the home was almost overwhelming, and at times you could walk into the house and it felt almost electrically charged. Claire and I were by now good friends and talked online daily. She suggested that I should try to cross over some of the spirits present in my home. I followed her advice, and before long crossing spirits over had become an almost nightly ritual, yet my home continued to fill back up with earthbound spirits and I began to wonder what on earth was going on.

On the day I finally got those answers I had been reading a photo posted by a member of an online group. One particular spirit present had caught my eye and was clearly visible to me in the photographs. He was wearing a leather jacket and had his blonde hair styled in a rather impressive Mohican. The following evening, I happened to take some photos of my own home and was astounded to discover that there was also a spirit in my own home wearing a leather jacket with a blonde Mohican! Surely not. That seemed far too coincidental. I messaged Claire, sent her the photographs and immediately she realized what was going on. When I was studying photographs, I was remotely removing the spirits I was reading. As the penny dropped, we started going through photographs I had taken in previous weeks of my home and cross-referencing them with readings I had done online. Sure enough, we recognized numerous spirits present in my home from earlier readings. I had been reading for hours a day online - no wonder I had a house full of spirits!

In no time at all, I discovered my next hurdle. My house was constantly full, and I was crossing over spirits daily, and for a while, the spirits I was dealing with were all earthbound spirits who actively wanted to cross over. But somewhere down the line I had started removing spirits of lower vibrations too, and not all of these spirits were so willing to cross into the light. One morning I woke up to see a woman with long dark hair standing right at the foot of my bed. I instantly recognized her from a reading I had done online a few days earlier. I tried to ignore her and go back to sleep but as soon as I closed my eyes and began to drift off, I had a vision. I saw a rope noose being held by my own hands. I then watched my hands loop the noose around my own neck, looked down to see a staircase at my feet and I threw myself forwards. I physically felt the sensation of my body falling before the rope tightened, jolting me awake. I looked up to see that the woman was still at the end of my bed. Clearly, sleep was out of the question until I helped her. She wanted to cross over but was too afraid, so I lay in bed talking to her and gaining her trust until she was finally able to let go of her fears and step into the light. She was the first of many and waking up to find a spirit in my room that wanted my help became a regular occurrence.

The months that followed proved to be somewhat of a steep learning curve, as I struggled to not only master these newly reawakened gifts but also to continue to juggle 'real life', a somewhat bewildered husband and four children. I can honestly say, that without their patience, and the unwavering support and guidance of Claire, that the outcome would have no doubt been a very different story indeed.

The more time I spent in various Facebook psychic groups putting my gifts to use and helping others, the more I realized what an absolute minefield these groups really were! So many were filled with such bad energy and negative interactions that I became frustrated with not being able to find a 'safe space' online in which I could offer readings without feeling like I constantly had to watch my back. One very cold rainy day just before Christmas in 2016, I decided to stop moaning about it and do something about it, and with the support of a handful of other readers I trusted, by the end of the day my group "The Psychic Hideaway" was born.

Soon after this I was approached by an online 'Psychic Seminary' and asked if I would consider teaching pendulum divination through their school. This proved to be a rather alarming encounter with an unethical organization which somewhat tarred my first forays into teaching the elements of spiritual development. I was horrified at the lack of integrity being demonstrated by this so-called 'psychic seminary'. I realized that I could not, in good conscience, have any association at all with those who found behaviors such as bullying and ridiculing students to be appropriate. I had gained so much insight and made so many wonderful connections with students through teaching, and I realized how much of a desperate need there was for a school of spiritual development that put the student's needs, ethics and acting with professional integrity at the forefront of their ethos. As a result of this realization, with the support and help of my now dear friend and mentor Clair Sage, in May 2017 I founded 'Liberatus School of Psychic Arts', an international online school of psychic and spiritual development. We offer a range of online courses and mentoring opportunities. Our aim is to create a safe and supportive learning environment in which students can develop and reach their maximum potential for spiritual growth.

I now work full time in this field, as a professional psychic medium, demonologist, shamanic healer, teacher, and mentor. For the first time in my life, I feel utterly at peace, knowing that I am finally fulfilling my life purpose in helping, healing and teaching others. Through this, I have been blessed enough to make some truly beautiful connections and friendships with both clients and students alike, for which I am enormously grateful.

With the current trend and prevalence of internet learning in our modern day and age, it has become more and more apparent to me that many issues in early development stem from the reliance on good old 'Doctor Google'. With access to answers at the touch of a few keys, those embarking on the journey of developing their gifts are in a very vulnerable position. Whereas in days of old, mentoring and development would be guided in person, we can now type anything into google and 'get answers. However, we have no means of validating their truth, we have no consistency, we miss out the absolute fundamental basics of protecting our own energy in a bid to jump ahead. We read dozens of conflicting statements and articles on any given subject and add to this the fact that everyone uses different terminology to describe the same things, and the same terminologies to describe different things and you can be left with a confusing pile of inaccurate, misleading, outdated or in some cases even dangerous information. This frequently encountered hurdle, along with numerous requests from students is essentially the inspiration for this book. A zero bulls**t, no-nonsense guide to embracing and developing your gifts, building strong foundations, doing so safely, and giving you the tools you need to begin reading for others using various forms of divination that can help to provide building blocks for both your skills as a reader and your confidence in taking that leap.

The truth of the matter is that each and every one of us have gifts. Every single one of us. All children are born with the ability to use their gifts by utilizing senses that go beyond obvious touch, sight, smell, hearing, and taste. As we get older, the majority of children will block off these gifts due to a number of internal and external influences such as fear, social conditioning, a desire to fit in, and in many cases simply a lack of understanding from the adults in their lives. There are only so many times you can be told that it is 'just your imagination' before you begin to believe that this is actually the case! The simple fact is that as a species we are inherently fearful of the unknown. This in part comes down to a basic need for survival and we feel safer within situations that are known to us and feel familiar.

The majority of us utilize only the tiniest fraction of our senses and live our lives relying only on the smallest percentage of that which we can actually access. This is our safe comfort zone. But there is so much more than this which falls just beyond the reach of our socially conditioned radar. I was once given a perfect example to help explain this concept which I will share with you now. "We don't dispute the fact that dogs can hear noises at a much higher frequency than us. Whilst a dog can hear a very high-pitched whistle from miles away, it can be totally inaudible to humans. Therefore, we cannot dispute the fact that there are perfectly audible sounds outside of our hearing range. With this in mind, how can we dispute the fact that there are tangible occurrences in relation to any of the other senses that are simply not within our natural range of vision, touch or smell?" Many, if not most of us are simply wandering through our lives stuck in our safe comfort zones, paying attention only to the obvious, and neglecting the fact that we are viewing only through tunnel vision and neglecting to recognize or connect with anything that is not tuned into our regular frequency. My brother in law also once presented me with a wonderful analogy regarding the question of how one could argue the case for opening ourselves up to the possibility of the paranormal. It's such a simple analogy but really stuck with me and I have used it time and time again in conversation - "We cannot see the wind, but it would be impossible to ever dispute its effects on the world around us".

Throughout this book, I hope to provide you with the methods required to not only begin opening up and tuning into these frequencies, but also to help you to lay solid foundations in order to enable this growth to take place safely. This book will provide you with a vast array of tools and techniques to assist you in your spiritual development, in addition to providing information on various divination methods that can be utilized in early development to hone your skills and develop confidence in reading for both yourself and for others.

Spiritual Protection

In every single aspect of our lives, we will encounter evidence of the absolute and indisputable truth that there is both light and dark in everything. In our relationships there will be ups and downs, in our lives there will be good times and bad. The people we meet as we go about our daily lives will not all be beaming rays of sunshine. Some people have only good intentions towards us, and others we will know instinctively not to trust. Then of course there are also those who will put on a wonderful show of their 'pure' intentions, only to turn around further down the line and stab you in the back. This is life. This is balance. The light versus the dark. There is no escaping this truth in our 'real lives', so I am always somewhat baffled when I meet those who seem so hellbent on utterly denying the presence of the dark when it comes to the spiritual world.

Very often in the spiritual community I come across people vehemently stubborn in their unwavering view that there is no such thing as 'negative energy' or stating categorically that negative spirits don't exist. This is completely illogical to me. Earthbound spirits are human spirits who are bound to this earthly plane and have not yet chosen to or have been able to cross over. They are human spirits, flawed just as we are. The majority of negative earthbound spirits genuinely mean no harm. They are of negative vibrations purely due to their current emotional state. Earthbound spirits that I work with are often confused, anxious, afraid, remorseful or fearful of judgement. Whilst they mean no harm, their vibrations are low, and because of this their presence can negatively impact on our own vibrations, regardless of their intentions towards us. However, as a wise man once told me, "spirits are just like people……. Some are lovely, some are 'alright', and some are outright jerks!". Yes! Some spirits ARE outright jerks!!! It is naive to attempt to gloss over this fact. A person who was absolutely vile, abusive, aggressive or mean-spirited in life, is going to be much the same in death, until they cross over into the light and are able to begin the process of healing.

In our 'real lives' as we go about our daily business, we have the advantage of being able to see, hear and be aware of exactly who, and what, we are dealing with. However, when we are learning to open up our gifts and embrace our spiritual and psychic connection, there will, of course, be times when we are working without the advantage of knowing with true certainty what is actually around us. For this reason, it is absolutely imperative that we always maintain a high level of protection against negative energies that may come our way. When we are reading for others we must connect to their energy, and we can end up inadvertently picking up negative vibrations and energies from them. This can literally stick to our aura as though it were pieces of dirt or lint on our clothing. Spiritual protection is particularly important for those with empathic ability, who will literally absorb the emotions and energy of others as if they were a sponge.

Perhaps the most essential methods of spiritual protection are grounding and shielding. Unfortunately, they also prove the most frequently neglected, these are two elements of what I often refer to as the foundations of spiritual development. Master these techniques early and practice them religiously and you will find yourself in a far stronger position with regards to both your own energy and your spiritual safety. I can honestly say that I had no idea that grounding or shielding were even 'a thing' when I was thrown blindly into my own journey of spiritual development. Oh, what a lot of drama I could have saved myself had I known! I recommend consciously practicing grounding and shielding techniques frequently. At least twice a day, before every reading, and throughout the day whenever you feel you have encountered, or are likely to encounter difficult people, energies or situations. The more you use these techniques, the easier and more natural they will feel, and before long you will find that they just become good habits that you instinctively use whenever they are needed. You may well discover that you are already doing one or both on occasion without even realizing it. As with most things, there is no right way or wrong way to do this - play around and find a method that feels comfortable and works for you.

GROUNDING

Grounding is an absolutely vital process before doing any type of spiritual work. Without it, your energy will be all over the place and you risk drifting off into airy fairyland. It is the most important spiritual practice you will ever learn. The more you practice grounding, the more aware you will become of how critical it is, not just for spiritual work and protection, but during our regular day to day experiences too. When we become ungrounded, we become scattered and lose control of our energy and emotions. To be grounded is to be centered, present and calm. Being grounded increases balance and stability in both our physical and emotional state. This in itself brings us strength and a sense of control. Being grounded helps in creating a bridge between spirit and matter, and assists in providing an outlet, making the release of energy easier. It also allows the attainment of higher vibrational frequencies and spiritual evolution.

The results of allowing your energy to become ungrounded can be surprisingly dramatic. There are numerous symptoms of becoming ungrounded and generally speaking, each individual will encounter the same few symptoms each time that their energy reaches this ungrounded state.

Dizziness
Daydreaming
A feeling of being 'Spaced Out'

BEYOND THE VEIL

Feeling sick
Heart palpitations
Eyes flickering
Weight gain
Clumsiness
Static shocks
Falling asleep when meditating
Becoming sensitive to noise and light
Becoming scatty or forgetful
Having brilliant ideas that never happen
Arguing frequently yet being unable to get your
point across due to lack of focus

In more extreme cases:
Blowing up light bulbs
Car troubles
Blowing fuses
Issues with all things electrical!

Whilst many of these symptoms may seem extreme, next time your electronics start going haywire and everything electrical starts playing up, pay attention to your own energy. You will be surprised at the effects we can have on technology when our energy gets out of control. I have experienced this to extremes on several occasions. One incident was a result of me becoming incredibly frustrated due to a disagreement with a friend. I had planned to spend the day getting to grips with my new tattoo machines. As soon as I began, my pedal broke, followed by the first machine. I switched my machines over to try the second. By now, my frustration was slowly increasing, and I was beginning to get angry over the situation. The second machine broke. Then the bulb went in my floor lamp. This blew the trip switch to the fuse box, which resulted in the house burglar alarm going off. Several swear words and a scream or two later, I finally had to see the funny side and burst out laughing. On another memorable occasion, the children had all been acting out for hours and were driving me crazy. The thing is when you have four children you are so dramatically outnumbered, that when things start to unravel it can become a little bit like trying to nail jelly to the wall as you try to get everyone to fall back into line! Split up one squabble, and before you know what's hit you another has broken out on the other side of the room! On this particular day, mummy had well and truly had enough! I had asked nicely, I had tried bribery, I had even resorted to threats of punishment and toy confiscation, and nothing was working. All around me there was shouting and squabbling and bickering and arguments over who was putting the toast in the toaster and why that wasn't fair and *'moan moan moan'* and then it happened. Mummy lost her s**t. As I opened my mouth and screamed, there was a loud bang and a shower of brightly colored sparks from the corner of the kitchen. I had blown up the toaster. Interestingly, this had a remarkable effect on my children! The moment it happened my two youngest boys had turned to stare at me open-mouthed in horror. "Do you see what happens when mummy gets angry?" I asked. Well seriously, it's four to one and I'm hideously outnumbered. I'd have been a fool not to use this to my advantage! "When mummy gets angry things blow up, so don't make mummy angry again, okay?!" For the remainder of that day, they were impeccably behaved and didn't put another foot wrong. Sometimes you just have to go with the flow and take the advantage where you can find it!

There are many ways in which we can make grounding ourselves, and centering our energy, a part of our daily practice. Diet can play a huge part in this. There are many foods that can directly help with grounding. Eating foods that literally grow in the ground are especially good. Root vegetables, leafy greens, and grains are excellent. Chocolate is also well known for its grounding properties. Seriously, I'm not making it up - chocolate helps us to become grounded!

Drinking plenty of water is good for us for a vast array of reasons, and one of these is grounding. Let's face it, water is good for us in so many ways that it's crazy to think how few of us actually drink enough of it. Drink more water! Taking time in nature is an excellent way to ground and connect to the earth. Getting away from the hustle and bustle of modern-day life, away from technology, and allowing ourselves time to 'just be present' in nature, surrounded by fresh air, trees, and wildlife, is an excellent way to ground yourself. Exercising is scientifically proven to release endorphins that can help to combat stress and calm us. This impacts on us positively as a whole and promotes calm grounded energy.

Gardening may sound like a slightly random suggestion, but when gardening you literally have your hands in the ground! Touching the soil, tending to plants and connecting directly to the earth is an excellent form of grounding. For the same reason, cooking can be another very effective method of grounding. I personally find that I am particularly grounded whilst mucking out our horses' stables. There is nothing quite like getting your hands dirty to ground your energy. Spending time with animals is a wonderful way to ground. Animals are so instinctually in tune with our energy, that we often automatically ground and center ourselves whilst around them. We are naturally calmer and more grounded in their presence. Caring for animals can also be an excellent way to practice grounding - mucking out stables every day has become almost meditative for me because it helps me to ground and center myself so effectively.

Carrying certain crystals with us, or even just holding them, can also be very beneficial to grounding. Red jasper, bloodstone, hematite, gold tigers' eye, carnelian, garnet, and amber are particularly effective grounding crystals. I personally wear amber at all times due to its grounding properties.

Meditation and 7/11 breathing are also fantastic ways to ground our energy. On several occasions after missing a few swings in his golf lessons, my youngest son was seen to throw his golf club on the floor in frustration. He would then sit cross-legged in the middle of the golf course, meditating for a few minutes, before standing up and continuing his lesson successfully. Even at the tender age of 6, Harry was able to clearly discern that his energy had become ungrounded, and that he needed to rectify the situation before proceeding!

Visualization of roots........ This is an excellent technique to use daily, but especially before doing any readings or spiritual work. You can do it outside standing barefoot on the grass, touching a tree, or even (as I do before every reading) whilst next to a small potted plant with your fingers gently touching the soil. Whilst using this technique it is important to have both feet flat on the floor. Close your eyes & take a few deep breaths (7/11 breathing is perfect for this). Start to imagine roots growing down from the soles of your feet into the earth. As those roots grow down, imagine them starting to fan out and spread, firmly reaching down and connecting your energy to the earth. Whilst your roots grow down into the earth, say the following chant:

"TO THE GROUND, I AM BOUND,
FEEL MY ROOTS REACHING DOWN,
TO THE GROUND, I AM BOUND.
FEEL THE WEIGHT OF THE STONE,
ONE WITH EARTH, FLESH & BONE,
TO THE GROUND, I AM BOUND"

Author Unknown

The more you use this roots visualization technique the more effective it will become. Practice really does make perfect!

SHIELDING

Psychic shielding is so important. Sometimes we can 'pick up' energy from other people without even knowing that we are doing so. Their moods or emotions can 'bleed over' onto us, leaving us feeling angry, sad, tired, depressed, or whatever other random emotions they happen to be feeling - and not actually knowing where this emotion came from. This is an especially important practice for those who have empathic ability. An empath will literally absorb the energy of others soaking it up like a sponge. Those with this particular gift must be especially mindful of shielding at all times if they are to successfully protect their own energy.

When working with spirit, we also need to shield ourselves against negative energies. Unfortunately, very sadly, people will also sometimes deliberately send negative energy towards us. With psychic shielding techniques, we are able to set the boundaries which keep out unwanted energy from others, and this can also simultaneously strengthen our own aura, keeping it healthy and protected.

There are many different variations on the method I'm going to teach you now. But essentially it boils down to us creating a bubble, or as I often call it, my 'hamster ball'. Visualize a bubble of light surrounding you, from the top of your head down to the soles of your feet. Visualize this bubble being made of an opaque light that no negative energy can penetrate. Inside this opaque white bubble, you are safe from negative energy. This can be hard to get the hang of at first, but the more you do it the easier it becomes. You can practice this visualization technique anywhere. Use this technique as a guideline. As with most things, you should always be led by your intuition first and foremost! If you don't feel that a white bubble is for you, then try a gold bubble, a lilac bubble, a glittery rainbow bubble...... what is important is that it feels right for you.

If you feel more comfortable and protected using something other than a bubble, such as a solid wall of stone or bricks, then go with your gut and do what feels the best and most comfortable fit for you. A former student of mine found visualizing a bubble a very awkward process, but felt very comfortable whilst alone, simply holding out her hand and stating *'no'* in a firm voice. She found that this method worked fabulously well within the confines of her own home, however, it was not a method that she could easily utilize in public without drawing unwanted attention to herself. We came up with a shielding method for her that emulated the forceful nature of what was currently working, but that was less vocal and 'obvious' for use in public situations. She now visualizes slamming down a metal shutter, resulting in a loud bang as it hits the floor. With just a little trouble-shooting, we can personalize techniques to suit our own personal preferences and needs.

It is also worth noting that shielding can be hugely beneficial to children who are displaying an awareness of their own gifts and surroundings. If we think outside the box, being mindful of the individual child's own likes and preferences, we can very easily bring these techniques down to a level that they can understand, whilst also making it a fun daily practice. For example, most young children are familiar with the world of cartoons. In the film *Frozen*, the main character is seen creating an impassable wall of ice around herself. Superhero fans may prefer to 'activate' their invisible forcefields. When it comes to children, simply putting things into a format that 'makes sense' to them, can help them to master these protection techniques very easily. This provides them with the tools they need in order to protect and defend themselves spiritually as they develop and grow.

RAISING YOUR VIBRATIONS

Raising your vibrations is absolutely critical in the quest for spiritual growth. We have already discussed at length why protecting your vibrations, and maintaining them at a higher frequency, is a crucial component is protecting ourselves spiritually from negative energies. However, higher vibrations are also enormously beneficial to our journey of psychic and spiritual development and growth.

Everything is energy. And all energy vibrates at different frequencies. Negative energies have low vibrations. Evolved spirits, such as your guides and positive energies, vibrate higher. For ease, let's imagine that we human beings vibrate somewhere nearer the middle of the vibrational 'scale'. As you begin to open up your gifts and connect with your guides, you will need to raise your vibrations. In layman's terms, you want to vibrate higher so that your energetic frequency is closer to that of your guides and of spirit. When your vibrations are higher, you get closer to the correct frequency. The closer you are to the correct frequency, the easier it becomes to connect with your guides and with spirit.

When it comes to raising your vibrations, think healthy living and you cannot go far wrong. Eating a balanced, clean, unprocessed diet, rich in greens and low in chemicals, is an excellent place to start. Removing as many chemicals and toxins from your life as possible will also help dramatically. Many of the techniques used for grounding are also relevant - time spent in nature, exercise and drinking plenty of water will play a significant role in raising vibrations, as will avoiding alcohol and substance abuse. Increasing your water intake can improve vibrations very dramatically. I frequently challenge my students to drink a minimum of three liters of water a day, and then I badger them relentlessly about it when they forget! It sounds like such an easy thing to do, but it is amazing how quickly we can slip into bad habits regarding our water intake. Drinking more water can make the most enormous difference, not just to your vibrations but also to your overall health. With such profound benefits to our appearance alone, you would think that we would all be far more dedicated to maintaining our daily water intake!

We cannot neglect to mention sleep here too. I have already touched on my own personal experiences with sleep deprivation and as I said then, absolutely nothing will push you to breaking point faster than exhaustion. Sleep is hugely important and getting enough of it can dramatically impact on our vibrations. For those who struggle with sleeping soundly, or even falling to sleep in the first place, there are many excellent sleep meditations available on YouTube. The 7/11 breathing technique can also be of enormous benefit in achieving relaxation and freeing us of all of the clutter that can swim around in our heads, preventing us from falling asleep.

Alongside these general 'self-nurture' aspects that relate to the raising of your vibrations, we must not overlook other external elements that can dramatically improve our vibrational state. Laughter, as they say, is the best medicine, and in this instance, it really holds some weight. Laughter is a fabulous way to raise vibrations, as are things like dancing, hugging, listening to happy, joyful music, and generally doing things that make you feel good. When you feel good, your vibrations are high. Another hugely effective way to raise your vibrations is through regular meditation.

MEDITATION

Meditation is a practice. And that is exactly what it requires. Practice! Here I hope to provide you with some of the tools required for you to be able to start incorporating meditation into your daily life and allow you to begin exploring the many incredible benefits that it has to offer. There are a million and one reasons to meditate. It is a fabulous tool with which we can help to combat anxiety and stress or help ourselves to find insight and focus on a specific issue in our lives. For many of us is also a huge part of our spiritual journey. It's how we often connect with our guides, are presented with information, and find clarification on issues that we are exploring or experiencing.

However, meditation can also be an incredibly daunting prospect. People are advised all the time that they should start meditating in order to develop their gifts. So, they try, and they aren't sure if they are doing it right. After a week they still don't feel that they have developed or fail to see tangible improvements, so they knock it on the head and think "well I guess it just didn't work for me" or "I'm no good at meditating". Occasionally they stick at it for longer, because they have heard all about the amazing visions and communications that others get during meditation. But they aren't getting these spectacular light shows or mind-blowing revelations. So, they try harder. They are frustrated. They then get disheartened, lose confidence and stop.... These are just two of the scenarios that I come across all too frequently. It is vital to remember that each person's meditation journey is unique to them. The focus must be on the act of meditation itself at the beginning. The rest will come, but when we chase it, we immediately interfere with the very essence of what we are trying to achieve.

Here are two short exercises that can be hugely beneficial in helping to lay the foundations of successful meditation. Finding our optimal position from a comfort perspective and learning to breathe more effectively in order to relax and clear the mind.

The first step to meditating successfully is to find your most comfortable position. Finding this position will maximize the benefits of everything that you do during your meditation practice. The second thing to try, once in your chosen position, is to practice a little breathing exercise known as 7/11 breathing, that you can utilize each and every time you meditate.

There are several different postures or positions that are commonly used during meditation practice. During meditation is essential that you find a position that is comfortable for you. This will result in you getting the most out of each session. The first method is being seated. In this position, it is important to have both feet flat on the floor, with your hands placed in a relaxed position on your lap. It is important in this position that your spire is absolutely straight and erect. This allows for the optimal flow of energy through your body and supports deep breathing simply by allowing your lungs, diaphragm, and airways the room they need to perform properly. For this reason, do not lean back into the chair but sit upright. I don't get on well with this position personally, because my legs are simply too short! Getting my feet flat on the floor in this position is uncomfortable for me and leaves me feeling quite precariously perched on the edge of my seat (unless I am sitting on one of those little miniature chairs commonly found in primary schools). This is clearly not ideal, so I avoid this position at all costs! Personal preference and comfort are essential in order to facilitate true relaxation.

Many people, myself included will often meditate lying down. This can be especially effective when doing chakra meditations because it allows you to use healing crystals and have them placed along the body. It is also the method I use each night when I meditate immediately before I go to sleep.

My preferred position for most meditations is the lotus position. Again, in this position, it is imperative that the spine remains straight and erect (no slouching!). Before you begin meditation there are some things you can do to maximize your experience.

Wear loose, comfortable clothing. You may feel comfortable for a few minutes wearing tight jeans but trust me when I tell you that after a while, physical discomfort can really begin to detract from your meditation.

Find somewhere quiet and free from distractions. Put your phone on silent or turn off notifications. Ensure that you won't be disturbed. If this space is tidy and clutter free this can also be a big help. It's much easier to clear the mind in a clear environment!

Try to avoid meditation on a full stomach or when your body is tired (or immediately following exercise).

Spend a few minutes finding your most comfortable position for meditation. Once you are in that position, and free from distraction, try the breathing exercise below. After a few breaths feel free to close your eyes. As your heart rate begins to slow, you can stop actively counting and simply be aware of the act of breathing. With each out breath imagine the tension melting away and leaving your body. You can do this exercise for any length of time that feels comfortable from just a few minutes upwards. The purpose of this exercise is to help you find a relaxed meditative way of being.

For many people, simply sitting in silence and focusing on breathing, whilst gently allowing the hustle and bustle inside their minds to slowly ebb away, leaves them in a calm meditative state. For others, guided meditations can be an excellent way to gain confidence in your meditation practice. There are many truly excellent guided meditations available for free online, and YouTube, in particular, is a great place to start in your search. I am particularly keen on those by Jason Stephenson, and frequently recommend his guided meditations to my students, not least because his voice is so wonderfully relaxing - there is absolutely nothing worse than sitting down to a promising guided meditation, only to find that the spoken voice in the recording grates on you like nails dragging down a blackboard!

7/11 BREATHING

How can something as simple as breathing lower emotional arousal? The answer is very simple, and once grasped, provides an extra layer of understanding which might encourage more of us to try this simple and effective tool to control our anxiety levels. Breathing techniques are not just 'mind tricks', they produce a bodily response that lowers your anxiety, clears the mind and relaxes the body in a very physical way.

Deep breathing techniques all have one thing in common, they work by stimulating what is known as the parasympathetic nervous system. You may have heard of the 'fight or flight' response. The parasympathetic nervous system is simply the opposite of that. Instead of getting you ready for action, deep breathing activates a natural bodily response that can be described as 'rest and digest'. Out-breaths decrease your blood pressure, dilate your pupils and slow your heart rate – lowering emotional arousal in the process. Practicing this breathing technique a few times a day will lower your overall stress levels in the long term.

It's important to realize that it's the out-breaths that stimulate the response, so it stands to reason that a breathing technique with longer out-breaths than in-breaths will be more effective at lowering emotional arousal and clearing the mind. Here is how you do it, and it is as easy as it sounds:

1 - breathe in for a count of seven
2 - then breathe out for a count of eleven

Make sure that when you are breathing in, you are doing deep 'diaphragmatic breathing' (your diaphragm moves down and pushes your stomach out as you take in a breath) rather than shallower higher lung breathing. If you find that it's difficult to lengthen your breaths to a count of 11 or 7, then reduce the count to breathing in for 5 and out for 8, or whatever suits you best, as long as the out-breath is longer than the in-breath.

Continue in this way for a few minutes or longer if you have time – and enjoy the calming effect it will have on your mind and body. An added bonus of 7-11 breathing is that the very act of counting to 7 or 11 is a distraction technique, taking your mind off your immediate concerns, and clearing your mind. It can be very easy to fall into the trap of saying to yourself 'right, I'm going to meditate, I must relax!'. If you are anything like me then this usually has a totally counterproductive effect. But, if you are counting, you can't be mentally writing a shopping list, or trying to remember what's in the cupboards for dinner!

This wonderful breathing technique is not only helpful when it comes to preparing for meditation. On many an occasion, I have escaped to the nearest bathroom and used this breathing technique for a minute or two when faced with a stressful or overwhelming situation. Any time I begin to feel that I need to 'take a moment', I will use this technique, and it can be an absolute game changer, especially for those with any form of underlying anxiety. Many of my students also use this technique daily and have found that it can completely halt the rising anxiety and bring them instantly back down to a calm and rational state.

BEYOND THE VEIL

Cleansing

DEALING WITH NEGATIVE ENERGIES IN THE HOME

Sometimes, despite your very best efforts, you cannot avoid the presence of negative energies around you. These negative energies can obviously come in the form of people or situations that are beyond your control. However, they can also present themselves in the form of negative residual energy, negative spirits, and demonic entities. Have you ever walked into a home or building and instantly felt chills or an uneasy sinking feeling in your gut? This is very often a sign of our intuition alerting you and drawing your attention to the presence of negative energies in a space. There are many situations where this is easily handled by simply grounding and shielding in order to protect your own energy with spiritual 'self-defense'. However, if you find yourself having an issue in your own home this is an entirely different matter. When people find themselves in a situation in which they are living amongst negative paranormal energies, it can have a hugely detrimental effect on their health and wellbeing.

The impact of living in a home filled with negative energies can be huge and quite overwhelming, and by the time many of my clients reach me they are close the breaking point. These situations often start small, with one or two negative spirits in the home. Even if these spirits mean no harm and are of negative vibrations purely because of their own emotional state and unresolved issues, their presence in the home does several things. Firstly, over time it lowers the vibrations of all those who live in the home because being in the presence of negative energy drains us and brings our own vibrations down. When a person's vibrations become low, this vastly increases the occurrence of numerous emotional issues and behavioral patterns. Lower vibrations increase our chances of experiencing feelings of depression and anxiety, and lead to a greater occurrence of responses such as miscommunication, arguments & anger issues. In addition to this, when we are living amongst negative vibrations, we become drained and sleep patterns are often affected. Add exhaustion and or sleep deprivation into the mix and this is where the situation often begins to spiral out of control. All of these negative emotions and behavioral patterns churn out even more negative vibrations, filling the home with huge amounts of residual energy. Like attracts like, and this cycle of negativity very often ends up attracting further negative spirits and even demonic entities into the space, in what can become a perfect 'feeding ground' for negative entities. In some cases, these situations will result in a person's vibrations becoming so low that it becomes very easy for a negative entity to attach itself to their aura or energy field. This then further perpetuates the cycle.

In situations such as this, the best advice I could possibly give you would be to seek professional help. And by professional help, I do not mean the 'medium up the road' or random strangers in groups on the internet. When I say professional help, I refer to a person who specializes in this area and who has a proven track record and references and testimonials coming out of their ears. The reason for this is that this type of professional will be far better able equipped to assess the situation thoroughly and accurately in order to identify exactly what they are dealing with before they even begin working on your home. Experience will ensure that they know what to look for, are able to differentiate between spirit and the demonic, recognize portals, and are far less likely to miss things. They will also be far more likely to understand that different types of negative energies require different treatment and handling. Most importantly, if someone doesn't know what they are doing they can antagonize the situation enormously, leaving you to live in the mess they have created whilst they get to go home and forget all about it.

As wonderful a resource as online psychic groups are, they have many pitfalls, not least when it comes to this particular topic. Time and time again I will see a post referencing negative energies in a home and I see the same advice churned out like a stuck record. "You need to smudge your home". This happens in almost every online group I have ever come across, and the worst thing about it is that the majority of those issuing this advice have never had a significant encounter with a negative entity in their lives. It's not advice based on personal experience and success. More often than not, it's advice that they have seen given so many times in groups that they quite understandably presume it to be correct, and it therefore gets passed on constantly. Unfortunately, in many situations, this is the worst advice that people could follow. People often get very cross when I disagree with them on this issue, believing that this is what they were always told, and they read it everywhere, so it must be correct, right? Do you remember how people also used to tell us all that the best treatment for bad burns was to immediately slather them in oil or butter? You get my point I'm sure......

Whilst the advice to use sage in such situations is undoubtedly the most common of inappropriate suggestions, I have seen countless instances of bad advice being given. When online, it is all too easy to forget that the person who has posted details of their situation is just that. A real person just like you and me. I have seen so-called readers tell people at midnight that they must wake up their sleeping children and leave their home immediately, or be told that they need to move, or 'get out of there NOW'. I cannot express how negative an impact this can have on both the person in question, who is actually living in this situation, but also on the situation itself. All that is achieved by this type of comment is to instill extreme fear, panic, and anxiety. Not only does this have a physical impact on the person who is being told that they are not safe, but if there truly are any negative energies present in their home, then it will only perpetuate the situation by creating a feast of negativity on which they can feed. Such statements and fear mongering are not only unnecessary, but also unbelievably unethical. In contrast to this, I have also witnessed some truly ludicrous advice being handed out, such as *"make a circle of salt around you"* - that was it – no elaboration on how, why or what to do next. Now, whilst salt does indeed have excellent protective qualities, this advice was issued to a person afraid of her home. In effect, this reader had confirmed her fears that there was something to be afraid of and that she needed to protect herself, but as soon as the advice was issued the person giving it vanished seemingly into thin air. This left a frightened woman on the other side of the computer screen, afraid, standing inside a circle of salt and thinking *'well what the hell do I do now? Stay here forever? I'm obviously not safe outside of this circle!'*. I have also seen advice that borders on hilariously poor. I came across one woman who had previously been informed that in order to deal with the demonic entity present in her home, she must "flick black stones at it whilst repeating the words 'go away'". Seriously. When responding to people online we must always be mindful of the fact that they are actually living in this situation. Unless you are giving good, sound advice, based on a thorough assessment of what is actually present, then always remain mindful of the potential consequences of your words for the human being on the other side of the computer screen.

Sage and smudging are an absolutely wonderful form of cleansing, if, and only if, the situation is appropriate and fitting. Sage smudging is a fabulous method of cleansing a space of negative residual energy. It is also a brilliant method to use when cleansing spiritual tools of performing daily 'housekeeping' and maintenance cleansing of your workspace. However, in a situation where there are multiple unknown negative entities present, following the advice to smudge the home with sage can aggravate the situation enormously. Imagine discovering an angry lion standing in your kitchen, remembering that you once heard someone in a bar telling a story about 'that time' he chased off a pesky feral kitten from his doorstep with a water pistol. Would you try to chase off the lion with a water pistol? Of course not! When we are dealing with unknown paranormal energies, we cannot safely presume that they are pesky kittens, because if you try to chase off a lion by squirting a water pistol in its face, there's a pretty good chance it's going to eat you. Safety absolutely must come first and foremost in these situations. It is quite simply not worth the risk of 'having a play around' and hoping for the best. I have seen the catastrophic results of this approach far too many times and they can be horrific and life-changing. Safety first, always. Find a recommended professional who specializes in this area. Not the medium down the road, not a paranormal team who want to come in with a bunch of gadgets and provoke responses, but a recommended specialist.

SELF DEFENCE & PROTECTION

Prevention is always better than cure, and there are numerous ways in which we can defend our homes and ourselves against negative energies.

Keeping our vibrations and the vibrations of our home high is a very effective form of self-defense. Remember, like attracts like. If the vibrations of your home are kept high, it simply becomes an uncomfortable place for negative energies to be. Removing the daily buildup of negative residual energy on a regular basis is a huge help in keeping paranormal negative energies away. They are drawn to negative residual energy and feed off it, so removing this on a regular basis, as part of your daily or weekly routine, can work wonders in improving the vibrations of your home. I often explain this to people with the analogy that if you don't want rats moving into your apartment you will make sure that you don't leave food on the floor. It's the same concept. Remove the 'food' source and your home becomes less appealing. Daily or weekly cleansing of the home can, of course, be done with sage smudging, but dragons blood is also a wonderful cleansing tool. This can be burnt as resin, incense or oil and is hugely effective in repelling negative entities. It's a little like 'sage on steroids' for this purpose, and I tend to have this burning almost daily in my home. Do not be put off by the name - it is not actually the blood of a dragon! Dragons blood is a dark red natural resin formed from tree sap. Be aware when purchasing dragons blood that many items marketed as being dragons blood are simply manufactured composites rather than the genuine article. I highly recommend the dragons blood products available from Melanie at *Out of the Void* – details of which are listed in the resources section at the end of this book.

Black tourmaline is a wonderful crystal to have in the home and has many properties that make it excellent with regards to spiritual protection. Black tourmaline purifies the space and has powerful abilities to clear negative energies by absorbing and purifying them, making it an excellent choice for the home and regular cleansing rituals.

Sea salt is also a very simple and underutilized cleansing tool. Simply sprinkling some sea salt in the corner of each room of the home can really help to keep on top of day to day residual energy, absorbing it and therefore removing it from the atmosphere. Sea salt is also the perfect cleansing tool when used in sea salt baths. Simply adding a handful of sea salt to your bath water, cleansing and soaking in it whilst visualizing the daily buildup of negative energy being washed away, can be an enormously effective method of cleansing yourself of the negative energy collected throughout the day. Spiritually cleansing ourselves in this way is so important. Imagine putting on a pair of white jeans, all shiny and clean and then leaving the house for 12 hours…… the chances are that these white jeans are going to accumulate bits of dirt, dust, lint, and grime as you go about your day. Now imagine that your beautiful clean shiny aura leaves the house with you in the morning. Just like your jeans, throughout the day it is going to pick up bits of spiritual 'yuk', from that guy you brushed up against on the train, from that lady at work with anger issues…. you wouldn't leave your white jeans dirty, so don't leave your aura in a mess either!

RELIGION & THE BIBLE

Now, religion is a very difficult topic to address in relation to spiritual development. I'm a huge fan of the quote from the wonderful Maggie Smith in *A Room with a View*:

> *"My dear, religion is like a penis.*
> *It's a perfectly fine thing for one to have*
> *and take pride in, but when one takes it out and*
> *waves it in my face, we have a problem"*

When it comes to religion and the Bible, it is simply not a case of whether you are religious, whether you believe in God, in organized religion, are a Buddhist, a Catholic or an Atheist.

People often get upset or offended when I state my informed opinion that reading a bunch of Bible quotes and passages will not necessarily help in any way to defend them against negative energies. They often presume that this is due to my own religious beliefs, which is funny in many ways because I am actually a Christian, an Ordained Minister and have so many bibles in my home that I lost count some time ago...... but I digress. The reason that I make this statement goes back to the simple fact that was addressed earlier in this book. Negative earthbound spirits were once people. They still have the same free will, the same emotional capacity, and the same beliefs as they did when they were living. If a person had no belief in God and no respect for the word of the Bible in life, then it is reasonable to presume that this hasn't magically altered simply because they are now in spirit. It would be crazy to think that you could walk into a bar mid-brawl, recite Bible passages at a bunch of inebriated angry men and that they would suddenly stop fighting and leave. It is no different a scenario when working with angry or aggressive earthbound spirits. They are not going to 'stop' or 'leave' in the name of God if they don't believe in him. The Bible holds no power over negative spirits unless they actually believe in it. When dealing with demonic entities the Bible holds far more weight, but as with cleansing, I would never recommend creating a situation whereby you are going into a situation uninformed or uneducated and directly challenging demonic entities.

As my dear friend, Jojo Ybarra once said to me at the very start of my spiritual journey, "honey, please don't taunt the demons!". This was sage advice! If in any doubt as to what you are dealing with, always seek advice and help from someone who is both experienced and capable in this area.

ST. BENEDICT'S MEDAL AND PRAYER

There is one particular religious item that I do recommend can be of huge assistance in our own personal protection. This is St Benedict's medal and prayer. This medal is one of the oldest and most honored medals used by Catholics and due to the belief in its power against evil is also known as the "devil-chasing medal." Sometimes carried as part of the rosary, it is also found individually. In widespread use after its formal approval by Pope Benedict XIV in the 18th century, the medal is used by Catholics to ward off spiritual and physical dangers, especially those related to evil, poison, and temptation. However, this does not for one second mean that this form of protection can only be used by Catholics. It is an incredibly robust form of defense and I often recommend learning this prayer to my students. I personally use and speak this prayer in Latin, which is what I recommend is done if at all possible. It's not terribly long or difficult to learn and I always feel that speaking it in Latin rather than using the English translation adds somewhat to its power and strength. Below you will find the Latin prayer followed by the English translation.

"Crux sacra sit mihi lux,
Nunquam draco sit mihi dux.
Vade retro Satana.
Nunquam suade mihi vana,
Sunt mala quae libas,
Ipse venena bibas!"

English translation:
"The Holy Cross be my light,
Let not the dragon be my guide.
Begone, Satan.
Do not suggest to me thy vanities,
Evil are the things thou profferest,
Drink thou thy own poison!"

On the reverse side of the medal itself, you will find the initials to the words of the prayer. In the cross, the initials C S S M L are seen down the vertical, with N D S M D engraved across the horizontal. Surrounding the edge of the medal's reverse side we see V R S N S M V – S M Q L I V B - an incredibly handy prompt if you ever find yourself tongue-tied and getting in a muddle.

78

SMUDGING

Reminder - do not smudge if you suspect the presence of a demonic entity or any particularly aggressive negative spirits. Smudging in these circumstances can greatly antagonize the situation and make matters much worse. This tutorial is what to do only after these entities have been removed, or if you are cleansing to deal with day to day residual negative energy.

There is nothing more effective than smudging to purify the energy field of a person, place or thing and remove negative residual energy. Smoke from a proper smudging clears the air. It removes bad energy, negative vibes, heavy feelings, and raises the vibrations of both the space and the people present. The proper use of sage smudging amounts to a good scrub of the auric body. Before you engage in a smudging ceremony, however, there are things you should know and practices to adhere to so that you will receive the most out of the practice of smudging. Here we will cover the use of sage for spiritual cleansing and negative residual removal.

Smudging with sage is a deeply spiritual practice and you must be prepared to treat it as such. This is incredibly important because subconsciously, when we are not taking a ritual or practice seriously then our intention is less pure, and intention is everything!

Create a quiet space before you begin. Do not over think it. Overthinking is the enemy here - we must feel it rather than think it. There is a great and very deep purity inside of you; this is the time to let yourself feel that. You are stepping into a sacred ritual. You are turning your back on the darkness of this world and turning into the Light of the Divine.

Smudging is appropriate to do in numerous situations. If you are feeling down, negative, stuck, or in a spiritual low place then smudging can be of great assistance in removing the negative residual energy on and around you which is holding your vibrations down on a lower frequency. When your house, property, or any place or space has been exposed to heavy and negative energies or painful experiences and even illness smudging can help to counteract the effects of this by clearing the residual energy left behind. Similarly, if you move into a new location, smudging is the ideal way in which to cleanse space of the psychic imprints of previous occupants. Using smudging as a means to cleanse second-hand items to remove psychic imprints of previous owners is effective in exactly the same way. After an accident or a close call in your car, smudge the vehicle inside and out to remove negative residual energy and energetic imprints caused by your own panic, fear, and anxiety that can attract more negative experiences.

Smudging can also be used as a form of spiritual defense, creating a protective barrier against outside negative influences such as neighborhood issues, escalating conflicts, or when you are expecting visitors with low vibrations in your home. The effects of smudging on raising the vibrations of the space can very effectively counteract any negative vibrations trying to seep into the home.

Because of the effects of smudging on raising our vibrations, when you want to make prayers stronger and feel more connected to spirit, smudging can help enormously by raising our vibrations and bringing us closer to the desired frequency that we are trying to reach. Smudging can also assist us in achieving a state of spiritual clarity by helping to clear the 'fog' that negative energy creates.

You will need a smudge stick sage bundle or loose-leaf sage. Sage, sweetgrass, and cedar combinations can be purchased in a smudge stick, but a bundle of plain sage on its own is perfectly fine. My personal preference is white sage, but there is a vast array of various sages available both in stores and online - as with most things, I recommend simply trusting your instincts and going with your personal preference and what you feel most drawn to. Loose sage is absolutely fine if that's all you have.

You will also need a fireproof bowl. Traditionally an abalone shell is used. Whilst these are absolutely beautiful, they are entirely optional, and if the only thing you have to hand is an old chipped saucer this will suffice! You will use this to hold under the smoking sage stick to prevent accidental burns from loose embers or to hold the loose, smoking sage. You will also need a cigarette lighter, or wooden matches (longer kitchen matches are best), a lit candle or naked flame - a gas hob can be very handy at times when organization skills have failed, and you are scrambling around desperately trying to remember where you put the matches.

Before You Begin open a good-size crack in the windows on each side of the dwelling you are in if possible. If not on opposing sides, then open at least one window anyway. If you cannot open a window, then open the doors wide enough for some airflow. The traditional theory behind this advice is that this opening allows the negative energy a gap through which to leave, however on a practical level smudging is incredibly smoky and trust me when I say that setting off all of the smoke alarms in your home at midnight when everyone is sleeping does not generally go down terribly well. My long-suffering husband will happily confirm this!

What matters most during this ritual is that you are focused and that your intentions are clear.

Holding your sage stick over a fireproof bowl, light the end of the stick until it starts to flame. Blow out the flame and continue to blow the embers until they begin to smoke. At all times keep the stick over the bowl and pay attention to any embers that may fall outside of the bowl. Safety must always be a priority when working with fire in any way shape or form.

You will want to hold both the bowl and the smudge stick in one hand if you can, so you can fan the smoke with your other free hand. Practice this technique a bit before lighting the smudge stick. It can feel a little awkward at first, but you will soon figure out a method that is comfortable for you.

If you are smudging a dwelling, begin at the front and work your way to the back. Being methodical about it will ensure that you don't inadvertently miss out any rooms or corners of the home. You will want to smudge all rooms, attic and basement, cupboards and closets, and especially all corners. Be sure to include the bathroom(s). Holding the bowl under the smoking stick, blow on the stick as needed to keep the smoke rising, and re-light the stick when necessary. You want to have a visible trail of rising smoke as you work. As you walk through the dwelling, use your free hand, or as is traditionally used, a feather or a smudging fan, to waft the smoke in each room. Go high and low, paying special attention to all four corners. Negative energy often collects in tight cramped places. Say a verbal chant or prayer, asking for the area to be cleansed and purified and demand that negative energy leave the space. The words that you speak are far less important than the intention behind them. Keep it simple and easy to remember. But as always keep in mind that if it feels uncomfortable for you it's going to be less effective than something simple and basic that rolls easily off your tongue. Even something as straight-forward as *"negative energy leave this place, only positive energy stay in this space"* will work just fine.

If you are smudging yourself, begin by holding the bowl and stick in front of your heart/chest area. Continue to focus on the intention that any negative energy be removed and that you are cleansed and protected, helped and healed. As with cleansing a space or thing, also silently give thanks that you are receiving this help. Wave the smoking stick up from your heart, over your head, down your face and neck, down shoulders, arms, to the ends of your fingers. Beginning again at the heart area, swirl the smoking stick around your tummy, pelvis, both legs and under your feet. Turn yourself around in the smoke so that your backside is also completely bathed in this sacred smoke.

Crush and grind the tip of the smudge stick into the fireproof bowl to extinguish the embers. As an extra measure of safety when you are finished, feel the end of the stick to make sure it is thoroughly cooled. Set the stick, inside the bowl, in a safe place away from anything flammable for a while. (A porcelain stove top in the kitchen is a good location to place the bowl until you are sure the stick is cold.)

Now you can close the windows and doors and begin to enjoy the raised vibrations and purified energy. You will usually feel the difference immediately. Finally, when you empty the bowl of smudge ashes or get down to a tiny stub of the stick and want to discard or throw out what's left, do not dispose of the sacred plant remainders into the bin or garbage. Instead, scatter the ashes and left-over smudge bits into a flower bed or under a tree offering it back to the earth with gratitude, so that it can provide nutrients back to the soil. This disposal method also symbolizes leaving the negative feelings outside of the home. This age-old sacred smudging ritual is one that I recommend making a regular part of your spiritual routine. Smudging the home weekly will help enormously to keep the day to day buildup of negative residual energy to a minimum. Learning the correct and proper way to smudge will bring purification into your spiritual body and surroundings.

CLEANSING OF SPIRITUAL TOOLS

Cleansing your spiritual tools, crystals, pendulums, and even tarot cards is hugely important. Without it, you can find yourselves lugging around a whole host of negative energy without even realizing it. If you have spiritual 'tools' that you have just acquired or ones that you have been working with such as oracle cards or a pendulum, or even wearing, such as a pendant, it is a good idea to give them a little energy cleanse at regular intervals.

Cleansing spiritual tools is so important because it gets them back to their original state of high vibrations. A place from which they can do their best work without being dragged down by accumulated negative energies. Simply put, absolutely everything has a vibration, which even includes emotions and physical objects. Negative energy, including negative emotions and physical pain, have low vibrations. Crystals, when they are at their optimal vibrational state, resonate at a high vibration. Low and high vibrations cannot exist together, so the crystals will help to raise the low energies to high ones. That high vibrational energy means that your health and overall well-being is increased. Crystals that you work with or keep with you often should be cleansed more regularly than the ones that may simply be sitting on your desk or in a box. I wear a huge number of crystals myself in the form of rings and pendants, and occasionally am guilty of forgetting to cleanse them as regularly as the other spiritual tools that I use. Boy do I feel the difference when I eventually remember and get around to cleansing them! There are many recommended cleansing methods that we can utilize for this practice.

Cleansing under a full moon is an excellent way to cleanse our tools and this is my preferred method and is done as a monthly ritual. The strong full moon energy actually lasts for 3 days, so it's ok if you miss the actual day of a full moon. You can catch those moonlight rays on the day before, day of, and day after a full moon. Your crystals will still get the energy even if it is cloudy or raining. Not all of us have the privilege of being able to leave our valuable collections outside directly under the full moon. The weather can play havoc with our intentions for full moon cleansing, as can animals. My dogs would destroy my trays of tools in a matter of seconds if I left them outside, and in the past, I had a student who dutifully placed her pendulum outside under the full moon to cleanse, only to have it stolen by a mischievous raccoon! There are several ways to combat these dangers. Here in the UK the weather often means leaving cards outside would be an absolute recipe for disaster, and for this reason, I will often set my tools up on a windowsill to cleanse under the light of the full moon. This method is just as effective as having them sitting outside, whilst also allowing me to keep my 'treasures' safe. Another method that many of my students living in warmer climates adopt, is to place their tools in a tray outside and place a large upturned glass bowl on top of them. This seems to defend them against mischievous raccoons relatively effectively and removes the worry of an unexpected light rain shower damaging cards.

SAGE AND INCENSE: Sage is another wonderful energy cleanser. You simply run your crystals through the smoke or waft the smoke over your crystals. Dragons blood is another incense that I highly recommend for this type of cleansing. The obvious benefit of this method is its ease and convenience, as it can be done at any time of day or night whenever it's required rather than having to wait for the lunar cycle to complete.

OTHER CRYSTALS: Not everyone has the required elements needed to use this method of cleansing, but it is a very effective method if you have other crystals in your possession. Your crystals or pendulums can be placed on top of an amethyst cluster, placed on selenite, put in a bag with a tumbled Carnelian, or surrounded by Clear Quartz Points. The high vibrations of the crystals will help to cleanse the negative energy that has built up.

BURYING IN THE EARTH: Mother Earth and her own vibrational energies can help crystals to re-tune themselves back to their original vibrations. This would work if you used a pot with soil in it, otherwise, you could run the risk of losing your tools and crystal in the wilderness unless you remember to mark where you buried them. Take into consideration if the crystal has little nooks and crannies that dirt could get trapped in. For this reason, you would not wish to use this method to cleanse crystal clusters for example. There are other many other methods available such as using sound, salt, sunlight, water, rice etc....... but those discussed above are the methods that I find most effective, and also the most convenient. All of these methods, when practiced regularly, can assist in your spiritual and psychic development enormously. These are the building blocks to creating solid foundations, on which your development and exploration into fully embracing and unblocking your gifts can begin. When you create solid foundations on which to build, you are not only giving yourself the best possible chance for growth and success, but also ensuring that you have a secure point to which you can return at times when you need to take a step back and reflect. This is itself can prove to be invaluable.

Spiritual & Psychic Development

No self-respecting guide to spiritual development would be complete without some sort of directory explaining commonly found terminologies and different variations of gifts. As you embark on your quest for spiritual growth there are a vast array of confusing and complicated terms that can leave people feeling a little overwhelmed. Try not to get too hung up on fitting your own gifts into neat little boxes. Labels are really quite unimportant in the grand scheme of things, but it can help you to focus on specific areas of development if you at least have some greater understanding of what all of these confusing names and terminologies relate to.

SPIRIT GUIDES

At the start of your spiritual journey, there is one thing that almost everyone is impatient about...... meeting their spirit guides. It is often viewed as being the holy grail of spiritual development at the beginning of your journey. Spirit guides are incorporeal beings that are assigned to us before we are born that help nudge and guide us through life. They're responsible for helping us fulfill the spiritual contract we make with ourselves before we incarnate. Your higher self helps select these guides, who help us while we are living out our incarnation.

Every single one of us has spirit guides. Some of us have many and others only a few. Some of your guides are with you for an entire lifetime, and others will show up when their expertise in a certain area is needed. Guides can be distant ancestors, angels, animals, or spirits with a specific skill set or area of expertise. They watch over us and guide us throughout our lives, often without us knowing it. What we think of as our 'intuition' is very often actually our guides giving us a hint or a push in the right direction. They cannot, and will not interfere with our free will, although they will often influence situations for our greater good.

BEYOND THE VEIL

As we start to open up and remove blockages that are holding us back in our spiritual development, we become more aware of our guides and communications with them become more free-flowing and almost constant. Not because we are necessarily getting more communication from them, but because we become aware of their presence and learn to trust this communication for what it is! Listening to more 'seasoned' readers talk about their guides can often give a very false impression of guide communication to those in the earlier stages of their spiritual journey. We will often talk about them as though they are 'real' people, inadvertently giving the impression that we sit around a table with them having full blown conversations over a coffee. This can place huge and somewhat intimidating expectations regarding meeting spirit guides on those who are yet to do so.

The truth of the matter is that once a relationship and channels of communication with our spirit guides have fully opened, they do become a very real presence in our lives. They become our friends, our confidants, the 'people' we go to in times of trouble, and our 'support team' when things are going wrong. This connection becomes so strong that they become very real and ever-present beings in our daily lives. Our strong and very deep connection to our guides often leaves us talking about them to other likeminded people as if they were 'actual' people.

The downside of this is that we inadvertently leave newer readers with unrealistic expectations. When so much pressure and misconception is placed in this area it can easily create negative blocks to guide communication and hinder people enormously in actually hearing and listening to their guides. People can develop such high expectations that they miss the subtle signs of communication that are already occurring, not realizing that this is, in fact, their guides.

All guides communicate differently, and all have different areas of expertise, different strengths, and differing personalities, just as we do. This communication can be very subtle, especially at first until we learn to trust it for what it is. Some guides will talk to us and many will do this in silence, putting words, phrases, or information in our heads. Others are very visual and will show themselves to us readily in our minds eye, in dreams, and during meditation. Others can be more 'camera shy' and show themselves less often. One of my guides communicates almost exclusively through ear pressures, and now that I understand and trust in this form of communication, I am able to have relatively lengthy conversations with him using this method alone. Ear pressures can be something worth paying attention to. Some people can experience a sharp pressure that is almost painful in one ear as a warning or when we are being yelled at to pay attention immediately. With signs and symptoms such as this is can be very beneficial to journal and just make a brief note of your experiences as they happen. Often it can take some time to understand what these things mean and having the benefit of being able to look back and observe any patterns can be a great help.

It is not at all unusual for people to suddenly meet or 'acquire' a new guide. As we grow and develop, we will often find new guides coming our way. These new spirit guides will usually have an area of knowledge or expertise that is likely to soon become relevant to our growth and development.

Opening up the channels of communication requires being patient and paying attention to the subtle cues and signs that you are receiving. With time, trust, and the progression of our own spiritual development these connections get stronger. When it comes to developing this relationship with your spirit guides, I frequently urge my students to 'allow rather than chase'. When we chase things, we are putting pressure on them. This can often lead to huge amounts of frustration and self-doubt, and you may inadvertently construct a metaphorical roadblock that will hinder your progress.

There are many ways in which our guides will communicate with us and below are a few examples:

Sending signs - Guides can arrange synchronicities to help alert you to something you need to see or know about. Pay attention to these when they happen.

Gut feelings - Guides can poke you in the gut when you're experiencing something they want you to pay attention to. Following your gut feelings is probably a good idea. Have you ever had this eerie feeling that something terrible was going to happen, but you couldn't quite put your finger on it? That might be a guide poking you in your gut.

Intuitive insight - Guides can send you flashes of intuition which may sound like a voice in your head. "Slow down!" and then you realize you were almost in a car accident. Or "He's lying to you." These are thoughts that appear to come out of nowhere, but which contain important information you'll want to notice. Many people tune out their intuition, but it's a valuable source of information.

Sending people into your life - Your guides sometimes get together with other people's guides and together they try to create a meeting between their charges. Perhaps you are thinking about someone from college and then see them in the supermarket later that day. Chance encounter? Probably not. Perhaps you were thinking about moving and you run into your old realtor friend in the gym. If it feels like a coincidence, consider that it might be more of a setup. I no longer believe in coincidences!

Arranging and nudging - Guides can also nudge you in the direction they want you to go or arrange for something to happen to you. For example, perhaps you're running late and can't find your keys. You get frustrated because you need to get somewhere on time. Suddenly, your phone rings and it's a really important call that you probably would have missed if you had found your keys earlier. Who do you think actually misplaced your keys? This is hard for them because you have free will. They can only arrange so much or nudge so hard. The more you can pick up on their clues, the better. Sometimes you just need to surrender to a situation that seems frustrating.

Wouldn't it be great if your guides could just call you on the phone and tell you what's coming in your future, or tell you to look out for a guy named Chris, or that your child needs you and you should get to them right away? For some people, that's quite nearly how it works. It just takes time and practice to be able to hear, see, or feel your guides.

Here are some ways you can work on increasing your connection directly:

Listen to your intuition - That little voice that tells you to "slow down" or "buy bread" or "pay attention" is a direct communication from your guides or higher self. Try listening to your intuition and see what results you get. Many people dismiss their intuition. It's not always pleasant. Do not mistake your ego for your intuition, however. If you're hearing thoughts like, "Don't bother asking him out, he'll never go out with someone like you" then that's your ego. Flick him off your shoulder.

Go with your gut - Following your gut instinct is also a manner in which guides try to direct you. If something doesn't feel right, it probably isn't. At the very least, use your gut feelings to protect and keep yourself safe.

Two methods that have always worked well for me are guided meditations and simply asking my spirit guides to show themselves as I'm falling asleep.

The second method of 'ask and you shall receive!', is how I met one of my own guides, and I have numerous students who have been surprised by the effectiveness of this method. When you are relaxed and falling asleep ask your guide to show themselves to you, or make their presence known. They may come to you in the form of a vision, or you may meet them in your dreams.

Do not put pressure on yourself or the situation. It may not happen right away, but it will happen eventually when the time is right, and your guides will know exactly when that is.

It is also worth noting a few other points here. Occasionally a person will acquire what we refer to as an *imposter guide* - an entity of negative vibrations (almost always demonic) that will impersonate a new or even current guide. There are some key things to be aware of in relation to this unusual situation. They say, "knowledge is power" and in this instance, this phrase rings particularly true. Our spirit guides absolutely have our backs, supporting, advising, and assisting us always. However, they also like to 'keep it real'. One of my own guides, Deon, rolls his eyes at me so often that I am sure they may fall out of his head one day. He will also happily tease me or laugh at me at times, very much in the manner of friendly banter. My dear friend Catrina has a wonderful guide who used to stand with her arms folded shaking her head and 'tutting' at her! However, whilst all guides have their own distinct personalities, and some are undoubtedly more serious than others, there are a few behaviors that true guides will be hugely unlikely to demonstrate. There are a few important 'red flags' to be aware of, and knowledge of them will considerably lessen your chances of ever falling victim to an imposter guide.

Genuine spirit guides do not judge. Deon may tease me, but he would never judge me. They will also not hold grudges. Several years ago, I acquired a new guide, Sam. Having not long before this been dealing with no end of spiritual f**kery, I had all but had enough and let's just say that I was rather unwelcoming. I wasn't prepared to trust him when I had just gotten everything nice and calm and settled, and rather than acknowledge the development of another 'problem' I very stubbornly refused to 'play'. I was quite happy with the guides that I already had, and I wasn't going to give a potential imposter the satisfaction of reacting to him at all. After a few weeks of this, I was lying in bed trying to go to sleep and Sam was just standing next to my bed - looking back, it is pretty funny. I was there lying in bed pretending to ignore him, and he was standing there just not caring in the slightest, as if to say "well…. two can play at this game". In frustration, and because I wanted to actually get some sleep, I got a little angry and decided that it was time to just deal with it. So, I tried to banish him. Repeatedly! (It is perhaps worth noting here that true and genuine guides cannot be banished – even I am not stupid enough to actually risk potentially banishing my own new guide whilst half asleep!) The point of this little tale is a very simple one indeed. Guides do not hold grudges! They may roll their eyes at us, but they will not hold things against us. Perhaps the biggest red flag with regard to imposter guides relates more to what they are telling us rather than how. A genuine guide will not feed the ego. If a spirit guide ever starts to tell you that you are 'special' or better than everyone else or makes out that you are invincible in any way and that nothing can touch you, or is constantly massaging the ego, then pay attention. This is very unlikely to be a real spirit guide. True spirit guides want what is best for us, and an over-inflated ego certainly fails to fall into that category. Whilst imposter guides are a relatively infrequent occurrence it is always better to be aware that they exist, so you have the knowledge required to spot the signs should it ever occur to you or anyone else around you. It may be unlikely to ever happen, but as I stated previously - knowledge is power!

In summary, yes…. meeting our spirit guides is often spoken of as being much like the holy grail of early spiritual development, but there genuinely is no hurry. Your guides are not going anywhere. Just relax about it and learn to listen and trust in the subtle communications that are already taking place. The more you listen, the more you will hear.

THE CLAIRS

This collective word phrase includes all types of psychic sensitivity corresponding to the senses: seeing, hearing, feeling, smelling, tasting, touching. A person with these additional senses is one who is considered to be a medium. The terms psychic, medium, and psychic medium can be somewhat confusing, but in hugely simplified terms, a psychic can read the energy of the living, a medium is able to communicate with spirit (literally becoming the 'medium' by which information can be passed from spirit to the living. A psychic medium is able to combine these two. As people begin to open up and become aware of that around them which falls outside of their tunnel vision 'comfort zone', they will often find that they have one or two of the clair senses that begin to become apparent and develop first. These gifts will often become the strongest of their clair senses, but almost all people who have a few of the clairs to begin with, will discover that they usually develop most, if not all of these senses over time, to varying degrees. These senses are referred to as clairvoyance, clairsentience, clairalience, clairgustance, claircognizance, and clairtangency.

CLAIRVOYANCE

Clairvoyance refers to clear seeing. To reach into another vibrational frequency and visually perceive 'within the mind's eye', something existing in that realm. A clairvoyant is one who receives extrasensory impressions, and symbols in the form of 'inner sight', or mental images which are perceived without the aid of the physical eyes and are beyond the limitations of ordinary time and space. These impressions are often more easily perceived in a relaxed state and during meditation, though many clairvoyants can obtain visual information regarding the past, present, and future in a variety of environments.

It is worth noting that clairvoyance is a gift that manifests in so many different ways for so many different people that as with most things spiritual, there really is no 'normal'. Whilst many clairvoyants will have this gift manifest primarily through dreams and vision, clairvoyance can also relate to seeing spirits or energy in real time, whilst fully awake and going about our normal day. Some clairvoyants can see spirits in physical form both in 'person' and through photographic images. Others may feel the presence of a spirit in a picture or a dwelling and their clairvoyance will manifest in the mind's eye, clearly showing them a visual representation of the spirit in question. Clairvoyance is a gift that can be developed and enhanced in many ways, and the oil painting technique can be a very effective way of strengthening your clairvoyance.

OIL PAINTING TECHNIQUE

This is a fabulous technique taught to me several years ago by my wonderful mentor Claire Sage.

When we come across a photograph and pause for a moment to quickly glance at it for signs of spirit or orbs, we often make the mistake of trying to find them quickly and focus on them with a hard intense stare. This method of reading photographs is going to be very likely to lead you to overlook a lot of vital information which can become crucial in a spirit photo reading.

In this method of reading spirit photos, there is a need to go against your instincts to a certain extent. Instead of focusing and staring at the photo with 'hard' eyes, you are going to be required to relax your eyes to a 'soft' focus and spend a few minutes looking at the photo from a higher perspective, allowing your eyes to adjust to the energy and the spirits within the photo. You are going to imagine that the photo is an oil painting. This technique can be enormously beneficial in developing your ability to read spirit photos.

You will at first want to spend a little time relaxing and take a few moments to ground and center yourself before allowing your focus to soften. Look at the image as a whole rather than picking out individual elements, as though you were viewing an oil painting from across a room.

The first thing you are going to want to note down is not what you see, but how the photo makes you feel. What sensations are you picking up, is it a good or a bad feeling? Do you feel any emotions or any physical sensations?

Continue looking at the photo for about 30 seconds to 1 minute; this time frame allows all of your senses the time they need to adjust and tune into the image. If you are spotting spirit already, don't focus on them just yet. Instead, treat them like a paint stroke on an oil painting for now as you allow your eyes to take in everything else too.

Next, start taking in the objects, colors, smells, interior design, or any possible sounds that you pick up on. If you are already able to communicate with your guide, they may well also be giving you some insight with regards to what the room is like.

Don't worry at this point about trying to determine the history or in-depth details of the room as this is not important at this stage.

If you are already noticing spirit in the photo, try not to immediately dive into trying to describe them or thinking it's a man, woman or child. What you see now is just the start. They are going to become more detailed over time

Continue to study the image with soft-focused eyes as if it was an oil painting, viewing it in peace and with calm centered energy. There is no need to hurry this process. You may start to notice that the spirits in the photo begin to become quite cartoon-like, and with practice of this technique they may start to 'jump' (not literally - no need to panic!) out of the photo, becoming almost three dimensional. They may even jump out in color, and you could even begin to make out their hair color or clothes

As you continue to view the image with relaxed eyes, don't be surprised if you suddenly start thinking of age, gender, and types of clothing, or even information about lifestyle or causes of death. Make a mental note of any seemingly random information that comes to you. Try not to doubt what you receive, but instead trust in it.

This technique is not limited to use on spirit photos of rooms but can also be used in psychometry with objects. You can make use of this technique when doing readings from photographs of people who are alive too, and in mediumship readings for people who have passed away. The more this technique is practiced the easier it becomes, and most of our students find that they have excellent results whilst using this method.

CLAIRAUDIENCE

Clairaudience refers to the gift of clear hearing - To perceive sounds or words and extrasensory noise, from sources broadcast from spiritual or ethereal realms, in the form of 'inner ear' or mental tone which are perceived without the aid of the physical ear, and beyond the limitations of ordinary time and space. These tones and vibrations are more easily perceived in an alpha state and during meditation, though many clairaudients can obtain verbal and sound-related information regarding the past, present, and future in a variety of environments.

Now I have to be honest here……. Clairaudience can be somewhat of an infuriating gift! Remember how we talked about vibrations in terms of radio frequencies? Well, radio 'static' can often go hand in hand with developing clairaudience, and this is something I often describe as 'fine tuning'. Often those developing clairaudience will hear this type of radio static, distant music or even on occasion some faint ringing in the ears. This can be hugely distracting and frustrating as you try desperately to 'hear better' and make out what is actually coming through. On rare occasions whilst half-asleep lying in bed I will experience the somewhat startling occurrence of a spirit suddenly shouting a random word or phrase in my ear. Just as with clairvoyance, clairaudience for many can also be heard exclusively with your inner ear, or inside your head. During early development, this can be hard to distinguish from your own thoughts, but over time it does become easier to differentiate between the two. Very often our guides will communicate through clairaudience and we soon learn to recognize their voices, intonations, and personalities coming through.

An example of this is something that happened to me 18 months ago. My beloved springer spaniel Molly had been put to sleep a week prior to this event following a massive stroke, and I had received the call from the vet's surgery to inform me that her ashes were ready for me to collect. As eager as I was to bring her home, I spent the entire drive there giving myself the pep talk "keep it together, keep it together, do not cry or lose your s**t". Needless to say, I walked into reception and promptly burst into tears, before taking a seat and continuing to 'ugly cry' in the corner for the next five minutes whilst I waited for them to bring her ashes out to me. When they called my name, I stood up and walked to the desk. All of the other people in the waiting room with their dogs looked away not really knowing how to respond to the blubbering wreck before them. The receptionist extended her sympathies and passed over the counter a fancy looking paper bag, containing molly's ashes in a box, some flowers and a sympathy card. I thanked her, turned around and headed towards the door. Halfway across the reception hallway my guide Deon pops into my head, and in his booming and ever sarcastic voice said, "now that's what you call a doggy bag!". That's Deon all over. When it all hits the fan, he turns into Mr. Funny and cheers me up. I was so shocked and relieved to be snapped out of my misery that I burst out laughing. Goodness only knows what the people in the waiting room must have thought - I didn't even dare turn around before running out of the door and back to my car!

CLAIRSENTIENCE

Clairsentience is the term given to the gift of clear feeling - To perceive information by a "feeling" within the whole body, without any outer stimuli related to the feeling or information. This particular gift can be slightly more difficult to define and identify because it is so closely connected with other

110

gifts such as empathic ability and intuition. Gut feelings play a huge part in clairsentience. Imagine that you walk into an old building or are shown a photograph and you instantly get that feeling of sickness in the pit of your stomach. You may feel extreme sadness, anxiety, or anger and feel suddenly uncomfortable in your own skin.

There are some very simple ways in which we can begin to develop and strengthen these gut feelings. Most importantly, we want to develop our trust in these feelings. One of the simplest ways is to use photographic images. Ask a friend to show you a picture of a person that they know. Look at the image for a few moments and jot down what you feel.

Write down anything that you feel even if you don't feel that it's significant. This could be as straightforward in the beginning as you simply determining whether you get a positive or negative vibe from the person in the picture. Or you may feel suddenly overwhelmed with an emotion such as anxiety, or anger. Once you have written these gut feelings down you can ask your friend to validate whether what you have picked up is accurate or not. The more you practice this exercise the more confident you will become in trusting your gut feelings. When developing clairsentience it can be incredibly helpful to keep notes.

We will often receive physical sensations that can provide us with very important information. When practicing mediumship this can become quite critical and prove a great assistance in putting together the pieces of the puzzle.

Often these physical symptoms can seem quite vague, but with practice, it becomes easier to recognize the messages that you are receiving. Chest pain, for example can be quite general, but with experience you will find that you can begin to recognize the difference between these pains, giving you a clearer indication of the message. For example, my chest gets tight, almost as though I am about to experience a panic attack when dealing with a spirit who has high anxiety. A duller ache and almost sharpness slightly lower down often signifies that a spirit had issues with the lungs. These physical sensations, such as a tightening around the throat, discomfort in the head, aches or tingling sensations should always be noted. With time you will likely discover that they begin to form a pattern that is clearer to interpret.

CLAIRALIENCE

Clairalience is the term used to describe the gift of clear smelling – To smell a fragrance or odor relating to a substance or food which is not in one's surroundings. These odors are perceived without the aid of the physical nose and beyond the limitations of ordinary time and space. This is often a gift that presents itself when spirit or passed loved ones are nearby. We will sometimes get a waft of scent that appears to come from nowhere. Frequently this is a familiar scent, of flowers, perfume, or cigar smoke. This is usually a sign that we are in the company of spirit and is often a very uplifting and reassuring experience.

CLAIRTANGENCY

Clairtangency is the term given to describe the gift of clear touching. This gift is more commonly known as psychometry. Clairtnagency enables us to handle an object or touch an area and perceive through the palms of one's hands information about the article or its owner or history that was not previously known. This information can be gathered through any of the senses and those with psychometry may experience emotions, see visions in the mind's eye, obtain general impressions of their history and of the energetic imprint that they hold.

When developing clairtangency, it is important to follow a few basic steps before beginning. Firstly is a good practice to wash your hands. This may sound a little silly, but when we consider that we will be reading energy through our palms, we want to ensure that any residual or unwanted energy that we have picked up throughout the course of our day has been removed. The second step I recommend is to rub your hands together to develop a generous flow of energy between your palms and fingers. Once you are holding the object, simply take a few breaths to ground your own energy and begin taking note of what you pick up. What do you see? Feel? Hear? Smell? Emotions are often the strongest to come through and therefore what is most intensely felt.

CLAIRGUSTANCE

Clairgustance is the term used to describe the gift of clear tasting. Those with clairgustance have the ability to taste a substance without putting anything in their mouth. This can often happen in conjunction with clairalience due to the fact that taste and smell are so closely connected.

CLAIRCOGNIZANCE

Claircognizance is the term used to describe the gift of clear knowing. This gift is without question of a doubt one of the hardest gifts to learn to trust. The claircognizant will 'just know'. They will know without reading, without connecting, and often seemingly without trying. For this reason, claircognizance can be hard to trust because in the early stages of development you can quite literally feel that you are simply plucking answers out of thin air. You have no tangible validation. Nothing to see or hear that backs up what you know, you 'just know', and often when claircognizance first begins to develop you have no idea how or why you 'just know'.

This lack of opportunity to validate this through the other senses such as sight or hearing can make this information particularly hard to trust. It often feels like you are throwing out random answers without giving any contemplation to the situation or even attempting to read a situation. Learning to trust claircognizance often comes down to the 'throw yourself over the cliff' method of just going with it. The more you trust in this gift, the more validation you will receive. The more validation that you receive, the more you will trust in your claircognizance. The only way to start developing this gift is to start listening to it.

CHANNELING

Channeling is a specific form of mediumship gift in which a person allows his or her body and mind to be used as a mechanism for etheric world intelligence to bring psychic information or healing energy to others.

When channeling, it is absolutely imperative that safety comes first, even if you are already highly skilled in this area. Unless you are unwaveringly confident in your abilities to discern exactly who or what you are in the presence of, I would suggest that you hold off on allowing unknown energies to enter your body. Channeling without discernment can leave you enormously vulnerable to the influence of negative energies or picking up negative attachments.

There are a few other forms of spirit communication that fall loosely under this category - Automatic writing and automatic drawing. I say loosely because generally speaking these practices should not entail channeling. The arts of automatic drawing and writing are ideally a method by which we open up and access our subconscious mind,

116

allowing our own subconscious thoughts and those of our higher selves to come through. The danger of these practices though comes when people inadvertently fail to set this as their intention, and instead allow themselves to become a channel for external energies. If attempting automatic writing or drawing it is imperative that your intentions for this are set clearly before you begin.

EMPATHIC ABILITY AND INTUITION

Empathic ability is, very generally speaking, the ability to sense and feel the emotions and energy of other people and your surroundings. It is almost entirely outward facing and concerned with things other than yourself. A person with empathic ability will absorb the emotions and the energy of others entirely unintentionally, almost like a sponge. Because of this, shielding is absolutely imperative for empaths to learn and to master.

Without shielding, the gift of empathic ability can cause people to become utterly overwhelmed and unable to determine which emotions and feelings are truly their own, and which they have absorbed from others.

Intuition, on the other hand, involves turning inward and consulting your unconscious mind and 'gut feelings' to assess and understand a situation. Whilst it absolutely relies upon absorbing and processing the world around you, but the final element is very much internal.

Therefore the assumption that people with high levels of empathic ability are equally as blessed with intuition is somewhat misguided. Empathic ability and intuition are two entirely distinct aspects of one's personality and should not be merged into a single trait.

Perhaps one of the best pieces of advice that I was ever given regarding mediumship was this: "Never forget that you are a 'medium" - 'an intervening substance through which sensory impressions are conveyed or physical forces are transmitted.' Your job is not to interpret or make sense of the information that you are provided with. Your job as a medium is simply to pass this information on to the person for whom it was intended." This is sage advice and something that we should always keep in mind.

Avoid the temptation to translate the messages that you are receiving. This is not your job, and in trying to do so you can inadvertently alter or even lose the entire meaning of the message you are being asked to pass along. Avoid watering down or 'fluffing up' the information that you are given. It is not your place to do so. Our role as mediums is to pass on the messages from spirit exactly as they are.

BEYOND THE VEIL

Chakras

As we have already discussed, one of the biggest challenges that we face at the start of our spiritual journey is that of raising our vibrations in a bid to bring our frequency closer to that of spirit and that with whom we wish to connect.

Developing your chakras can be a relatively easy shortcut to enhancing your psychic abilities. Just by opening and clearing these energy centers of the body, a natural result of this will often be an enhanced psychic awareness.

When our chakras are open and balanced, our self-observation and connectivity expand organically. We have seven main chakra energy centers that run in a straight line along our spine – starting at the base and ending at the crown of our head. When our chakras are open and vibrant, we are abundantly rich in the vital life force, known in Sanskrit as "Prana." We feel grounded, inspired, energized, loving, kind, grateful, intuitive, and connected to source and spirit. When energy becomes stagnant in one or more of these vortexes, we are prone to experience emotional congestion fueled by fear, limiting beliefs, and lack of self-love – which opens us up to emotional, physical, and spiritual pain.

Opening our chakras energizes us, and awakened chakras promote emotional and spiritual growth. We experience "free-flowing" energy and information that moves in alignment within the natural rhythms of our bodies and the universal rhythms of nature.

The seven major chakras, from the base of the spine to the crown are the root chakra, the sacral chakra, the solar plexus chakra, the heart chakra, the throat chakra, the brow chakra, and the crown chakra. Each of these chakras is related to numerous physical and emotional attributes.

The Root Chakra is the red chakra located at the base of the spine. The Sanskrit name for this chakra is *muladhara*. It is associated with our connection to earth, survival, health, abundance, family, passion, and moving forward in life. If the root chakra becomes unbalanced, you may feel physically and emotionally "stuck" and unable to move forward in life. You may feel ungrounded, with a depleting sense of self. Blockages within the chakra are frequently associated with traumatic events, the death of a loved one, family or relationship problems and major life changes. A blockage in the root chakra prevents the release of grief, guilt, and sadness. This can contribute to the inability to move forward and prevent you from feeling able to follow your destiny. Common emotional symptoms of an unbalanced root chakra include feelings of loneliness, insecurities, feeling ungrounded, having a lack of confidence, feeling that you have been abandoned, indecision, depression and anxiety, problems with addictions, suffering from phobias and obsessions. Common physical symptoms of an unbalanced root chakra include lower-back pain, sciatica, varicose veins, constipation, diarrhea, rectal/anal problems, impotence, water retention, and issues with groin, hips, legs, knees, calves, ankles, and feet.

The sacral chakra is the orange chakra located at the base of the spine. Its Sanskrit name is *svadhisthana*. The sacral chakra is associated with our connection to other people, to creativity, the flow of energy, confidence, and sexual health. If the sacral chakra becomes unbalanced, you will most likely have a noticeable lack of energy flow throughout the entire body. You may feel extremely lethargic and unmotivated with regards to life in general, but particularly in relation to exercise and sex. Blockages in the sacral chakra often lead to feelings of sadness, loneliness, and mild depression. Common emotional symptoms of an unbalanced sacral chakra include eating disorders, issues with addiction, low self-confidence, dependency issues, low libido, and unbalanced emotions. Common physical symptoms of an unbalanced sacral chakra include things such as kidney problems and urinary tract infections, chronic lower back pain, sexual disorders, infertility, gynecological issues, dysfunctional menstrual cycles, and problems with the intestines, spleen, and gallbladder.

The solar plexus chakra is the yellow chakra located at the diaphragm. The Sanskrit name for the solar plexus chakra is *manipura*. This chakra is associated with our physical center, personal power, desire, inner-strength, emotions, instincts, and "gut" feelings. The solar plexus chakra is also hugely impacting on issues surrounding self-doubt. If the solar plexus chakra becomes unbalanced, you may feel very stressed all of the time and also feel somewhat helpless regarding your ability to regain control. This can often leave people feeling mentally and physically exhausted. You may have "gut" feelings but are not sure of what or where they are coming from which can often contribute to your distress and discomfort. The stress of an unbalanced solar plexus chakra also very often contributes to poor memory and concentration. Common emotional symptoms of an unbalanced solar plexus chakra: lack of memory and concentration, feeling frequently fearful even when this is not logical in relation to the given situation, feeling uncentered, sugar addictions, insomnia, and eating disorders. Common physical symptoms of an unbalanced solar plexus chakra include digestive and intestinal disorders, food allergies, eating disorders, poor metabolism, diabetes, obesity, eczema, acne, and other stress-related skin conditions.

The heart chakra is the green chakra located in the region of the physical heart. Its Sanskrit name is *anahata*. The heart chakra is the center of your spirit as well as the center of the chakras, making it a vital energy center for our spiritual, mental, emotional and physical well-being. The heart chakra is associated with love, compassion, trust, adventure, safety, self-love, forgiveness, and relationships. If the heart chakra becomes unbalanced, you may feel experience feelings of detachment from the world around you. Every single breath we take that connects us to our physical and spiritual world is enveloped by the heart chakra, and if this becomes unbalanced or blocked it can lead to a disconnection from the people we love as well as a loss of love and compassion for ourselves. Problems in relationships often become heightened and we often begin to lose hope. We can also lose sight of love, beauty, empathy, and compassion. Common emotional symptoms of an unbalanced heart chakra include a tendency to become apathetic, losing faith, becoming unforgiving, feelings of hopelessness, becoming increasingly distrustful, a lack of commitment, and a sense of detachment. Common physical symptoms of an unbalanced heart chakra include chest problems such as pneumonia, asthma, breast problems, respiratory problems, upper-back pain, shoulder and upper-arm pain, and premature aging.

The throat chakra is the blue chakra located at the base of the throat. The Sanskrit name for this chakra is *vishuddha*. The throat chakra is associated with communication, freedom, expression, responsibility, and leadership. If the throat chakra becomes unbalanced, you may feel you are unable to communicate verbally, physically, and emotionally. The throat chakra connects us to our ability to express ourselves and therefore creates a vast array of issues if it becomes blocked or unbalanced, particularly in relation to subconscious attitudes or feelings becoming trapped and unable to surface. The throat chakra can often become closed due to severe trauma which subsequently makes in incredibly difficult for people to verbalize and communicate their feelings. Common emotional symptoms of an unbalanced throat chakra include feelings of nervousness, anxiety, fear, feelings of isolation, attention deficit disorders, and poor coping skills. Common physical symptoms of an unbalanced throat chakra include problems with the nasal area, irritated sinuses, sore throat, jaw pain, physical voice loss, thyroid problems, tissues with the teeth or gums and ailments of the esophagus and tonsils.

The brow chakra is the indigo chakra located between and just above the physical eyes, in the location of the pineal gland in the center of the brows. This chakra is sometimes also seen as being gold or white in color. Its Sanskrit name is *ajna*. This chakra is often also referred to as the third-eye chakra. The brow chakra is associated with the mind, ideas, thoughts, intuition, dreams, and psychic abilities. If the brow chakra becomes unbalanced, we can feel bombarded and overwhelmed with our own thoughts and become unable to process them effectively. We may also feel stuck in an emotional and intellectual rut. We lose our sense of intuition, which leaves us feeling that our judgment is clouded, and this can often cause us to make poor decisions. When the brow chakra becomes blocked, we can also become closed off to new ideas and fall off the paths of our true destiny, instead choosing to remain in our comfort zone. Common psychological symptoms of an unbalanced third-eye chakra include headaches and migraines, nightmares, seizures, neurological disorders, personality disorders, neurotic behavior, learning difficulties, and hallucinations. Common physical symptoms of an unbalanced third-eye chakra include suffering from eye problems, glaucoma, issues with hearing or the ears, spinal conditions, and problems with the scalp or hair.

The crown chakra is the violet chakra that is located at the crown of the head. The Sanskrit name for this chakra is *sahasrara*. The crown chakra is associated with the Divine and higher powers, spirituality, divine wisdom, enlightenment, connection to the universe, optimism, imagination, and awareness. If the crown chakra becomes unbalanced, we can feel spiritually disconnected and as though we are living without any direction or purpose. If a person has many physical ailments and diseases that seem to continually resurface without an obvious root trigger or cause, then it is highly likely that an unbalanced crown chakra could be the cause, as this chakra affects the six energy systems below, and is connected to your entire being. A blocked crown chakra can lead to depression and nervous system disorders in addition to feelings of being lost and incomplete. Common psychological symptoms of an unbalanced crown chakra can include depression, confusion, loss of faith, feeling mentally disconnected, dementia, epilepsy and schizophrenia. Common physical symptoms of an unbalanced crown chakra often include issues such as light sensitivity, frequent headaches, dementia, autoimmune and neurological disorders. The crown chakra affects the health of our brains as a whole and is therefore connected to our entire state of mental, physical, and spiritual health.

Investing some time in chakra health can often have quite dramatic effects, not only on your physical and emotional wellbeing, but on your psychic and spiritual development. Guided meditations can be of huge assistance in this area.

Trusting your Intuition

As you embark on your journey of spiritual and psychic development, learning to actually trust in your intuition is arguably one of the greatest hurdles that you will face. Without building this trust in your intuition it is almost, if not completely impossible to nurture and develop the confidence required to successfully develop your gifts. Working so closely with so many different students over the last few years has made it abundantly clear to me that the best and only logical way in which to start developing this trust in your intuition is to actually start reading, firstly for yourself and then for others.

The more you practice your reading skills, the more in tune you will become with your intuition. The more you read, the more validation you will receive, and the more validation you receive the more your confidence and trust will grow. This positive cycle of psychic development enables you to gain confidence in your gifts, in yourself, and in the information you are receiving from your intuition, from your guides and from spirit. However, getting started with this can seem like a vastly intimidating a scary process and many people find the prospect incredibly overwhelming, especially when they have no idea where to begin. In this section of the book I have included some information on some of the reading methods that I consider to be the most straightforward and rewarding with which to begin the process of developing as a psychic reader. These forms of divination are excellent options to explore when you first begin nurturing and developing confidence in your gifts.

As with most things in life, everyone will be drawn to different areas of divination and you are likely to find that one or two of these divination forms feel more natural and comfortable to you than others. Some forms of reading will very quickly 'click', almost as if you already knew them before you started, and with others, it will soon become apparent that they are just not for you. The information provided below will take you through how to get started, however as always, stay mindful of the fact that there is no right or wrong way here - experiment and explore in your own time, developing your own methods that feel most comfortable and natural to you.

ORACLE CARDS

Now I have to be absolutely honest here…. I used to be of the opinion that oracle cards were pretty pointless. I loathe tarot - not because there is anything wrong with it, but it's just not for me. As you begin to develop your psychic gifts you will find that you are often incredibly drawn to some things whilst others hold absolutely no interest for you whatsoever. Due to my disinterest in tarot, I pretty much wrote oracle cards off as being of no use to me. How wrong I was! Oracle cards have gained some serious momentum in popularity because of the fact that there's no set structure for how each oracle deck is created. Anybody can create an oracle deck and assign to it whatever purpose and outline they want, limited by nothing but their imagination. With this capacity for creative input, combined with such a vast array of amazing designs, it wasn't long before the artist in me started admiring the wonderful artwork in some of these decks. I decided to treat myself and purchase a deck that had caught my eye, thinking that I should at least have a play around before I wrote them off completely. So many of the client cases that I take on are very heavy going and dealing so frequently with so many negative energies can be pretty draining, so I figured that if nothing else I could have a play around with something pretty whilst I recharged. Within a few minutes I was hooked, and before I knew it, I had accumulated quite the collection of oracle decks.

Oracle cards are an absolute joy to use, often alarmingly accurate in their insight and arguably the best method of providing readings for yourself. When you combine this with the fact that there are so many beautiful decks available and they are so simple to use it becomes difficult to question their suitability as a starting point for anyone wishing to develop their intuitive skills and delve into providing readings.

When deciding which deck is right for you, you will hear time and time again the phrase "pick the ones you are drawn to". Often people are concerned that this means they need to go shopping, handle a bunch of different decks and be expected to know which ones are the right ones for them. I genuinely do not feel that this is necessary. It's very much like the old superstition that a tarot deck must be gifted to you. There is no question that once upon a time this would have been the case. A tarot deck would have been passed down from one psychic to another. We don't live in those times anymore. Back in the day, tarot decks were not readily available, spiritual stores were few and far between and this was often the only way cards could be acquired. Times have changed, and there is absolutely nothing wrong with purchasing your decks online. You can be drawn to a deck that you stumble across on Amazon just as easily as you can be drawn to a deck physically in front of you in a specialist boutique. There is absolutely nothing wrong with buying decks online. If you like them and are excited by them, then you are drawn to them!

Oracle decks are wonderful for any short-term type of questions that require you to do some inner reflection and soul-searching. Tarot cards are more suited to long term issues and questions that address your overall life journey. Short term questions such as "what should I focus on at this time? Or "What is holding me back?" are absolutely perfect for oracle card readings.

Oracle cards are arguably one of the best spiritual tools for giving yourself an intuitive reading. I often draw an oracle card for myself when I feel that I need a little spiritual kick up the backside or if am struggling to see the wood for the trees. In actual fact, using oracle cards to read for yourself is probably the best possible way to connect and bond with your deck and to learn trust in the process. Once you are comfortable reading for yourself with oracle cards it is a relatively easy and straightforward progression moving onto reading for others.

Whether you're checking in for guidance on yourself, a friend, or a client, here are a few tips on how to get the most out of your cards and enable you to take things to the next level.

Select your deck wisely. When purchasing decks, follow your intuition and choose ones you feel particularly drawn to. Most people find that they end up collecting decks over time. This can really pay off as you will find that different oracle decks will speak to you depending upon numerous factors such as your current mood and circumstances or those of the person you are reading for.

BEYOND THE VEIL

Once you get your new oracle cards home it is always wise to cleanse them just as you would any other spiritual tools. Sage smudging is perfect for this purpose unless of course, you happen to have timed your purchase in line with an upcoming full moon! Once your cards have been cleansed take some time to bond with them. Hold them, shuffle them, carry them around with you…. this will help to attune them to your vibrations.

Treat your decks with respect. When doing a reading for a friend or client, you should always be the person who shuffles and picks the cards. This prevents anyone else from touching your deck and as a result, protects them from anyone else's energy. Once you have finished using your cards, immediately put them back in their box or pouch and ensure to put them away in a safe place. Decks can be well-worn and well-loved, but they should always be respected. The more you care for the energy of your deck, the more accurate your readings will be.

It is simply not necessary to ask specific questions. Whilst I will often ask my guides what it is that I need to know right now, I do so more out of habit than necessity. Your higher self and your intuition will always know exactly what it is that you need to know most at any given time. The result of this is that more often than not, the issues that we believe to be the most pressing are very often not those that truly are. Try to approach the cards with a blank, open mind - ensuring that you ground, shield, and take a few moments to breathe and relax, will help enormously with this. When reading for yourself, make sure that you're alone in a quiet place where you can relax and tune in effectively to your own energy. If reading for someone else, simply focus on the energy of the other person as you shuffle the cards. Find your shuffling method. There are many ways to pick individual cards from a deck in order to provide a reading but having a play around with different methods and experimenting until you find the one that feels most comfortable and right for you will play an important role in you gaining trust in yourself and confidence in the cards. I often like to shuffle the deck until a card flies out of the deck dramatically. But I do sometimes go for a more 'controlled' approach (having a puppy in the house can make the first option slightly risky!) and I will shuffle until my intuition leads me to stop. I will then cut the deck allowing my intuition to guide me. Other people may simply pick the card on top of the deck at that moment. Play around and see where your intuition leads you and what feels right for you personally. You can use any traditional tarot spreads with oracle cards, such as the Celtic cross or the three-card spread (representing past, present, and future). However, many oracle decks will also have their own creative variations of different spreads in the instruction manual and it is always fun to try these out and see how they feel for you. Of course, you do not need to rely on spreads, and can simply draw a single card from the deck or continue to draw individual cards until your guides and intuition tells you to stop. You may instantly know what number of cards to pull, but there is nothing wrong with just continuing to slowly pull cards until you feel the cue to stop. As with all methods of reading and divination you can be as traditional as you wish, or simply go with whatever feels right to you. There is no right way or wrong way to use oracle cards, and as long as the basic rules relating to cleansing and treating your cards with respect are adhered to, you really can follow your intuition and go with what feels right to you.

Your first intuitive feelings when you look at each card are very important. Whilst most oracle cards come complete with instruction or guidance booklets that outline the detailed meaning of each card, the images on the cards themselves can hold just as much importance. Consider your first thoughts regarding what a card means for you or the person you are reading for. Your gut reaction to cards is often just as important if not more so that the meaning detailed in the instruction booklet.

The information in the booklet that will likely come with your cards is not necessarily the most important or vital thing to consider. Whilst it can be informative to read the detailed entries and descriptions relating to each card when you get a new deck, your own intuitive interpretation of the cards meaning is equally as important. Many oracle cards will have one short, general message or phrase that gives a general overview printed on the card itself. Always listen to what your own intuition is telling you about the card in relation to either your own situation or your clients. Remember that the entries in the book are guidelines only. Lastly, it is important to be mindful not to use oracle cards (or any other form of reading for yourself such as pendulum divination) as a crutch. If you find that you are constantly giving yourself readings several times a day, the accuracy rate will plummet. Some people like to draw one card for themselves daily, others only once weekly, or when a specific issue has arisen that they feel they would benefit from some guidance on. As with all forms of divination, you will soon develop a natural rhythm that feels comfortable and works for you.

Pendulum Divination

PENDULUM DIVINATION IN HISTORY

Pendulum divination is one of the oldest methods of receiving guidance from the spirit world. There is no recorded information on the introduction of pendulum divination, but most cultures have some form of seeking help from the spiritual realm. A French priest reportedly employed the use of pendulum divination very successfully during the early 1900s. He located water, minerals, and missing people using maps. The Vatican is said to have hired him to locate several lost treasures. This was especially significant since Pope John XXII banned the use of pendulums during the 1320s, declaring that the answers were coming directly from the devil.

Ancient Egyptians believed that the pendulum was magical. Romans had a belief in the pendulum as a reliable tool to receive divine guidance on the problems that they faced. A favorite choice of the pendulum historically was to tie a wedding ring to a strand of hair or fine piece of string or thread. One of the most commonly asked questions was the sex of an unborn baby. If the ring moved in a circular motion, the baby was believed to be a girl. A straight line either back and forth or sideways indicated a male child. Pendulums were also used in deciding where to plant the future year's crop. The Chinese used pendulums to determine where evil spirits were hiding in order to chase them from the home. Pendulums can be used to locate portals, provide psychic readings, for medical diagnosis, healing, to pinpoint locations, to pinpoint timeframes, to locate ley lines, to assist in finding underground crystal crops, to verify cards in a tarot reading........ even to perform a tarot reading without any cards being present.

The pendulum can be an extremely useful tool for elaborating on any number of readings, allowing you to obtain further information from your higher self and to expand on your initial impressions.

HOW DOES A PENDULUM WORK?

Thought moves the pendulum. Thought directs the subconscious as to the direction in which the pendulum is to move. The subconscious uses the brain to send signals along the neurological pathways that control the muscle "twitches" that move the pendulum in the desired direction. We can use a pendulum to gain information from the subconscious mind, the body and cells of the body, the higher self (the intuitive spiritual part of yourself) and also from other spirits.

When spirit communicates with us using a pendulum, these responses come from the subconscious mind. Spirit is not physically moving the pendulum. Spirit answers through the subconscious. Each time we use a pendulum, we are tapping into the subconscious and connecting with our intuition, our guides, and our higher self. When used correctly, this makes the pendulum a wonderful tool for unblocking psychic abilities.

The challenge of using a pendulum is to clear your mind completely of conscious and unconscious thoughts regarding which direction the pendulum will move in, and in which direction you want it to move.

One of the easiest, quickest, and most effective ways I have found to do this is by using the 7/11 breathing techniques discussed previously in this book and ensuring to ground yourself properly before using the pendulum.

CLEANSING YOUR PENDULUM

It is vital that we cleanse all of our spiritual tools before we use them. Monthly cleansing under the full moon is an incredibly effective method of cleansing our pendulums. However, it would be unreasonable to expect people to purchase or handmake a new pendulum and not use it for weeks whilst awaiting a full moon!

To cleanse new pendulums upon purchase and for daily cleansing, I recommend using either white sage or dragons blood incense for convenience, although you can, of course, use any of the other methods of cleansing already mentioned within this book.

BONDING WITH YOUR PENDULUM

When you cleanse your pendulum, you are removing all accumulated negative energies and restoring its natural vibrations. Once this is done it can be hugely beneficial to 'bond' with your pendulum, tuning it to your own specific energy and vibrations. This can be done in many ways, such as holding the pendulum in your hands, carrying it around with you or even sleeping with it placed underneath your pillow. Many of my female students prefer the method of popping their pendulums into their bra when they are busily going about their day so that they are in constant physical contact with it, and this is a method that works incredibly well!

HOLDING YOUR PENDULUM

There are several recommended ways to hold your pendulum. In my option, there is no 'perfect' method, as each of us will have different preferences. As long as the basics are adhered to, I recommend experimenting a little to find what works best for you. If you are uncomfortable, you will be unable to relax, and this will be detrimental to your end results.

The end of the pendulum should be gripped between the thumb and either the forefinger or the tip of the middle finger. It is important that this is a pincer grip (between the fingertips) rather than the end of the pendulum being squashed between two flat finger pads. The fingers should be held horizontally, with the pendulum hanging down vertically. I cannot stress enough how important it is that this grip is relaxed. The desired outcome is that our own energy can flow freely. Tension will almost always prevent this energetic flow, so a firm (to prevent dropping the pendulum) yet relaxed grip is essential.

Many people recommend that the elbow is rested on a table top or flat surface whilst using a pendulum, to ensure that to hand is kept still and therefore 'unable' to influence results. However, I do not feel that this is necessary, and I do not personally rest my elbow on a surface - not least because I have very short arms, and this often results in my pendulum hitting the crystals and clutter on my desk! Again, this comes down to you experimenting and finding what works best and is most comfortable for you.

PROGRAMMING YOUR PENDULUM

Programming your pendulum is actually a very straightforward process. The purpose of doing this is to learn how to decipher the responses you are given, and to determine what the movement from your pendulum is telling you.

Begin by following the steps above, ensuring that your pendulum is thoroughly cleansed and charged with your energy. Then take a few moments to ground, shield, and clear your mind using the 7/11 breathing technique described earlier in this book.

Pick up your pendulum and make sure that your grip is relaxed and secure. Then simply ask your pendulum to show you a '*yes*' response. Make a note of the direction in which your pendulum moves. Does it swing clockwise? Anticlockwise? Back and forth? This is your '*yes*' response. Take a moment to clear your mind again, and now ask your pendulum to show you a '*no*' response. Again, make a note of the direction in which your pendulum swings. Do the same for a '*maybe*' response. Do keep in mind that the responses can differ for different people. Whilst I get a clockwise response for '*yes*', anticlockwise for '*no*', and back and forth swing for a '*maybe*', there is no right or wrong here, so do not panic if you discover that your own responses differ from mine or anyone else's.

Once you have determined the responses your pendulum gives, you can build on your confidence in handling your pendulum by asking other questions such as '*am I married*? *Do I have children? Is my middle name Doris?'*. As you become more confident in using and trusting your pendulum, you will likely find that the responses you get may become stronger as your nerves lessen, and you become more relaxed.

IMPROVING ACCURACY

Next, we must extend this programming to ensure that we are getting the truth, free from any negativity or dishonesty. It's time to elaborate on our programming and set our intentions. In order to do this, we must carry out the second phase of calibration. Ask your pendulum the following questions, setting your intent in the process. *"Pendulum, do you agree to tell the truth, and only the truth?"*. If your pendulum responds with anything other than *'yes',* or stands still, keep on repeating the question until it does give a *'yes'* response. Confirm this by saying: *"Pendulum, you agree to tell the truth and always the truth, correct?"* You should get another *'yes' response*. Next, say: *"Pendulum, do you promise to seek answers from only my higher self, and from positive energies?"* You should get a *'yes'*, if not, keep repeating until you do. Then confirm by asking: *"Pendulum, will you seek answers from negative energies?"* You should get a *'no'*, if not repeat. Then: *"Pendulum, will you seek answers from my conscious mind?"* You should get a *'no',* if not repeat. Then ask *"Pendulum, will you seek answers from entities of lower vibrations?"* You should get a *'no',* if not, repeat. Confirm all of the previous questions. Finally, ask this question: *"Pendulum, do you agree to bring answers only from the divine light, and only from sources that are good and not negative, bad, harmful, or malicious in any way?"*

You should get a strong *'yes'* response. If not, then repeat all of the other questions before asking this one again, before confirming the final question. In asking these questions, what you are doing is setting clear intentions within the conscious mind which will enable you to receive the optimal performance from your pendulum.

WORDING IS EVERYTHING

When using a pendulum, wording is everything. This cannot be stressed enough. As a reader, you will find that around 95% of the questions you get asked by a sitter during a pendulum reading will need rewording. Failure to do so will lead to inaccurate and frustrating results.

When asking questions, always begin with the phrase *"all things considered...."*. This phrase invites your higher self to look at all relevant facts and reasons in order to get the best possible response.

When asking questions regarding choices to be made, begin by asking *"all things considered, is it optimal......."*. This will help you to get the best possible answer regarding the question being asked.

There are several key points to keep in mind when asking pendulum questions. Ask one question at a time! You are using a divination tool that provides simple *yes/no/maybe* responses. To get the most out of this tool we need to break things down. For example........ during a reading you are asked: *"will I be successful in my current job or not & if I stay will I get a promotion soon?"* That's a whole lot of questions and we are going to need to break it down before asking our pendulums in order to ensure accurate results. For example:

1)*Will 'X' be successful in her current job?*
2)*If 'X' stays in their current position of employment will they get a promotion?*

Now the querent, (the person asking the question) has asked if a promotion will be *'soon'*. That is very much a *'how long is a piece of string'* type question. However we can elaborate on this. If the answer to question 2 is yes....... take it further. Will they get a promotion within the 6 months? One year? Two years? You can easily give them a much clearer time frame than *'soon'*.

By thinking through the question presented to you thoroughly, you have developed your one-word answer into something far more coherent. For example, rather than *'yes/no/maybe'*, we have something more like this...... (obviously, this is based on a make-believe scenario & answers): *"I am getting/being told/picking up that you will be successful in your current employment situation, and that a promotion could well be on the cards for you in the next 9-10 months if things continue on their current path"*

Sometimes you will be asked a question that is far too general. For example...... *"Will I meet somebody soon?"*. The answer to this question is going to be *'yes'*. Why? Because *'soon' could* mean this week or next year. Most importantly, *'somebody'*, means anybody! I am almost certainly going to meet *'somebody'* tomorrow.... I'm going to meet a few mums in the playground, I'm going to meet the person at the checkout in the supermarket, I'll probably meet somebody in a field mid-morning when I'm walking the dogs! So, as a reader, we need to clarify whether the person asking this question actually means a love interest (this is invariably the case, but always clarify rather than presuming). If they are referring to a love interest, then this is what we ask, whilst elaborating on the *'soon'*.

There is something else that is critical to understand when providing readings. Nothing is set in stone, and free will is everything. Free will is usually addressed by the maybe response from our pendulums. For example, someone asks you the question: *"I'm doing slimming world at the moment, and I want to know if I am going to get down to my goal weight?"*. You get a response from your pendulum that is a *'maybe'*. Why? Because their success is based on free will choices. If their free will takes them to McDonald's every morning for breakfast, and they choose to eat pizza every evening for dinner, then they are unlikely to succeed. If they do follow the suggested exercise and nutrition regime that had been set, then they are most likely to succeed.

But nobody can influence or alter their free will. And free will can turn on a dime.

Free will is a very important thing to keep in mind during readings. Because it can change an outcome in an instant. For example, you are asked: *"am I going to get married to my current boyfriend?"*. Your pendulum gives you a *'yes'* response. Amazing! Congratulations....... but wait. 2 weeks later one of them gets intoxicated and carried away at a party and cheats on the other. The other partner chooses to end the relationship as a result. Wedding off. So was your answer wrong? No........ at the time you did the reading, on their current path's course they were headed for marriage. Free will has changed that course, and this is something that is out of our control completely. For this reason, when answering pendulum questions always think to mention the impact of free will. Just because my pendulum says today that a person is in line for a pay rise, that doesn't mean that they can bunk off work and go to Ibiza for a month partying because their promotion is set in stone. This act of free will would completely alter their path's direction and therefore change the likely outcome of their future.

BEYOND THE VEIL

Aura Reading

Everything radiates an aura, whether it is a person, an animal or an object. The frequency of energy that radiates out helps to create the energetic field around us, and each differing frequency manifests itself as a different color in the aura. The color of an aura will not remain the same throughout a person's lifetime; it can change frequently depending on their emotional state and their spiritual advancement. It is not terribly unusual to even notice the color of a person's aura change over a very short space of time, sometimes even from one minute to the next, as the energetic field is affected by every thought and interaction that they have.

Learning to read auras can not only be fun, but once you have the hang of it you can also use this skill to add extra depth and assist yourself in gathering additional information in almost all types of psychic readings that you do. The colors that radiate in an aura can often reveal much more about a person than that person will ever care to admit about themselves. It is not difficult to notice and see an aura and it only requires a little effort and patience. This section of the book is going to address the basics of how to see and read auras.

Be aware of energy. Before you can fully begin to develop your ability to see auras, you need to first become more aware of how energy feels in your body. Next time you are with a friend, try to pay some attention to how you feel in their presence. Do they invite you in to feel pleasant emotions or do they drain you of your energy? Take a few moments to ground, shield, and focus on aligning yourself with your own breath and ask for an honest sensation of how they make you feel.

Objects also have auras. To begin seeing the aura of an object, gaze at one spot on or just next to the object for 30 – 60 seconds and allow your gaze to soften. Notice those objects just outside of your direct sight; there is no need to strain or stress. Remember to breathe normally while practicing this soft-focus vision. You should start to see that many items have a white or silvery type of aura that surrounds the whole object.

When you are ready to move on to see the aura of a person, please try to get their permission first. This helps with being able to have easier access to seeing their aura, especially if you are new to seeing auras, and ethically speaking it is always paramount that people's privacy and boundaries are respected. Ask them to stand 14 – 18 inches in front of you against a neutral colored wall. A white or cream background works best for this exercise. Look at the wall next to the person and focus in on their energy field. Softly gaze through them and at the wall around them. You can ask the aura to show itself to you and pay attention to not only your vision but also your sense of the colors. Once you have made this connection in reading the aura, you can move up to the next stage by asking the person to move around slowly to see if you can still sense the same colors.

Once you have developed your skills by reading the auras of others, you will be ready to be able to try reading your own aura. This can often be a little bit more challenging than reading the aura of others, but it is a good way of strengthening your intuitive abilities. Sit in a quiet, meditative space and clear your mind. Set an intention that you would like access to see your aura. Gently rub your hands together as this activates energy between the two hands. Focus your attention between the palms and see if you can sense or see your aura color. It may take 30 – 60 seconds for you to see your aura. If you are not able to see your aura on your first attempt, please don't be put off! It can take many attempts before you eventually do see it. As with most things patience and practice is key. Seeing auras is just one step to greater awareness and elevating our consciousness.

AURA COLOURS

Each color that we can see in an aura is linked to a different frequency, and each frequency relates various information about the person in question. Below you will find a brief guide on what these colors can tell us about a person.

RED AURAS

Red Aura people are enthusiastic and energetic individuals, forever on the lookout for new adventures. They are adventurous with food, travel, and sexual partners. The red aura individual tends to have an "I'll try anything once" attitude to life. Because of their more daring approach to life they can often find themselves in hot water. Red aura people are quick to anger and can lose their temper over the slightest thing. But on a more positive note, they are usually generous with their time and energy when called upon for help. They are usually strong in both mind and body and do not succumb to physical or mental illness easily. Because of their robust health and fitness, the red aura individual likes to be physical and will usually excel in sports.

People with a predominant red aura color can easily become bored and need to move on to different interests, projects, and relationships, and as a result often leave numerous unfinished ventures in their wake. But, if they set their mind to a project and can stick to it, they will have remarkable success and can become extremely wealthy. Red aura people are usually direct, to the point and forthright, and are not afraid to make their point of view known. They don't normally have hidden agendas or ulterior motives. What you see is what you get with the open and upfront red aura individual. Above all else the red aura individual needs to be number one. They are competitive by nature and the need to 'win' will drive them towards great success in life. They are often not good team players and won't take orders from others so will often prefer to run their own business or take on a role of authority over others.

YELLOW AURAS

Yellow aura people are analytical, logical, and usually very intelligent. They tend to excel in careers that involve teaching and study and make excellent inventors and scientists. They can often have a tendency to work too hard, be overachievers and can easily become workaholics by failing to maintain a work/life balance, instead choosing to put their work above personal relationships. Yellow aura people are most often perfectly happy to be in their own company and do not crave the presence or company of others. They are often prone to mental health pressures and sometimes become withdrawn and depressed when stressed. The yellow aura individual has excellent communication skills and can display this on a one to one basis whilst doing so equally as proficiently to large crowds. They are confident in their abilities to get their ideas and messages across and tend to be a great inspiration to others.

Yellow aura people have very good observation skills and can read people easily. They are usually extremely perceptive individuals. They will not suffer fools gladly and will choose their few friends carefully keeping their circle small. Friends they do have will need to match the yellow aura person's wit and intellect.

The yellow aura individual tends to lead with their head over their heart when making difficult choices or decisions. They are often quite unorthodox and unconventional in their thinking and are not afraid to experiment with unusual or 'off the wall' ideas and original concepts. The yellow aura individual often seems a little eccentric with unusual interests and hobbies. They are attracted to things that are considered avant-garde, intellectual or unusual. The most common 'flaw' of a person who has a predominant yellow aura is that they can be overly critical of themselves and others.

PINK AURAS

People with pink auras are by nature very loving and giving. They love to be well loved too and will often gather close friends and family around them at every possible opportunity. They like to host family events and are very generous of their time. They also tend to place high levels of importance on their health and physical wellbeing and will, for the most part, look after their bodies with good diet, nutrition, and exercise. Pink aura people are romantics, and once they have found their soulmate will most often remain faithful and loyal for life.

The pink aura individual is a natural healer, highly sensitive to the needs of others and has strong psychic abilities. They also tend to have very creative ideas and strong imaginations. Because of these specific personality traits and skill sets those with pink auras make great writers of novels, poetry, or song lyrics.

The pink aura individual loathes any instances of injustice, poverty, and conflicts. They have a strong desire to make the world a better place and will often make vast personal sacrifices in the pursuit of this ideal. Pink aura people are strong-willed and highly disciplined and will expect high standards from others. They have strong values and morals and seldom deviate from them. Their loyalty and loving nature make them wonderful friends, and their honesty and likable nature means that they are generally highly valued as both employees and also as employers because of their inherent sense of fairness.

GREEN AURAS

Green aura people are highly creative and very hard working. They constantly strive for perfection in almost everything that they do. They tend to be highly determined individuals but maintain a down to earth nature and will not allow elaborate dreams and unrealistic ideas to color their world. Their creativity takes the form of practical matters such as gardening, cooking, and home decorating. The green aura individual has an eye for detail and will ensure that their appearance and clothing, home and surroundings are both practical and beautiful.

Green aura people tend to be very popular, admired and respected by others. They tend to be very successful in business and can create and manifest great wealth and prosperity for themselves. Green aura people like security, stability, and balance in their lives. They plan carefully and seldom make rash mistakes. Close friends of those with green auras will be treated to generosity, loyalty, and practical advice. They do not suffer fools gladly and generally choose their friends very carefully. People with a predominant green aura are likely to be health-conscious and ensure that their diet is nutritious, balanced, health-giving and tasty. They are always in tune with nature and love the great outdoors.

ORANGE AURAS

Orange aura people are social butterflies that love to be in the company of others and are happy being the center of attention or just another face in the crowd. As long as they are surrounded by others, they are happy. They want to please others and tend to be very thoughtful and generous. The orange aura individual is usually kind-hearted and honest. They are very much tuned in to the emotions of others and can sense and feel their pain and joy.

Orange aura people can be very charming, but part of their charm is in their sensitivity to others. They have the ability to make everyone feel at ease in their company. The orange aura individual can on occasions be hot-headed and quick to lose their temper, but on the flip side of this, they are equally quick to forgive and forget if a sincere apology is offered and accepted. They seldom hold grudges. They tend to lead very successful and happy lives. Those with orange auras tend to be impatient and have a tendency to rush into projects, relationships, and experiences too quickly. They often act immediately and consider the consequences after the fact.

PURPLE AURAS

Those with purple auras are highly psychic, well attuned to the emotions and moods of others and are incredibly sensitive. People who have a predominant amount of purple in their aura are often seen as being very mysterious and secretive. The purple aura individual possesses a philosophical, curious, and intuitive mind. They love to learn and rarely stop exploring and enquiring into new subjects and areas that interest them. They are constant seekers of knowledge. Because of this they tend to be extremely interesting and knowledgeable people.

The purple aura individual keeps their circle of friends small, but the friends that they do have are held incredibly close and are truly respected, admired, and loved. People with a predominant purple aura are often unlucky in love but once they have found their perfect soul mate, they are incredibly loyal and loving for life. Purple aura people usually connect well with animals and nature. They are highly attuned to animals and can sense their emotions and feelings. Purple aura people will often take in and care for strays as their loving and caring nature makes it difficult for them to turn them away.

BLUE AURAS

Having a predominantly blue aura or energy field surrounding you can indicate a number of personality traits. Entirely blue auras are quite rare but can occasionally show up as one of the boldest aura colors in people with strong personalities. Blue aura individuals are the master communicators of the world. They have the ability to clearly convey their thoughts, ideas, views, and concepts both eloquently and with incredible levels of charisma. They make excellent writers, poets, and politicians.

Blue aura people are also highly intelligent and intuitive. They usually have the head and heart balanced when making difficult decisions or choices. They are also incredibly good organizers and can motivate and inspire others with ease. People who have a predominant amount of blue in their auras are natural peacemakers due to their ability to speak calmly and rationally. They value honesty, truthful communication, and clarity in relationships. The downside of the blue aura personality is that they can often take on too much and neglect their personal relationships as a result.

GOLD AURAS

Gold aura people are lovers of beauty and are often blessed with a very artistic flair. They tend to appreciate the finer things in life and like to adorn themselves and their homes with exquisite items of beauty. They love to entertain and prefer the company of many. They do not feel intimated by being the center of attention and they often actually thrive on it. The gold aura individual tends to be very focused on appearance, are often attractive and love to attract attention, affection, and admiration from others. Because this the gold aura personality will usually have a large number of friends. But they are not just takers of time, affection, and attention; the gold aura individual will also give generously of their own time, energy, and love to others. The charming and charismatic nature displayed by the gold aura personality only adds to their attractiveness. They are also great listeners and can make anyone feel comfortable, important, and interesting in their company.

Gold aura individuals hate to be criticized and cannot stand any of their flaws being exposed. They are often overly lavish and have a tendency towards being materialistic. They strive always to impress, give the most generous gifts and host the most impressive social gatherings, even if their budget will not allow this. They are very proud and fiercely independent and often find it extremely difficult to ask for help from others.

SILVER AURAS

Those with silver auras are often exceptionally gifted. Silver aura individuals are bestowed with high levels of sensitivity, intuitiveness, psychic ability, and practicality. They can use their spiritual understanding in very practical ways. Because of this they can relate to many people and are often found in teaching, mentoring, or counselling careers.

People with silver auras tend to have immense versatility and adaptability and are capable of getting the most out of practically any opportunity presented to them in life. Their high intellect allows them to make wise decisions quickly and follow through with appropriate action. People who have predominant silver auras are generally considered attractive by others. They often attract many admirers, but silver aura people are also very discerning and choose their friends and partners very carefully. Silver aura individuals are usually blessed with being physically attractive. They also overflow with personality and talent and because of this they are seen as incredibly lucky people. Success often appears to come very easily to those with silver auras.

BROWN AURAS

The presence of brown in the aura is generally considered to be of negative consequence. It is important however to keep in mind that this is not always the case. In rare instances, a 'warm' brown hue can be an indication of somebody who is highly grounded and connected to the earth.

However, in the majority of cases, a brown aura will be more of a 'muggy' looking brown in color. If this is a lighter brown in color, then it often indicates confusion or discouragement. Those displaying a light brown aura tend to be experiencing a lack of confidence and vast amounts of self-doubt in relation either to their current situation or in the subject being addressed. Those displaying a 'muggy' dark brown aura often do so in indication of selfishness, constant fault finding, and a tendency toward deception.

BLACK AURAS

Those with a black aura are showing indications of hatred, negativity, serious ill health, depression, and misery. This color being present in an aura is always a bad sign.

Palmistry

The history of palmistry is uncertain; however, it is widely believed to have originated in India before eventually finding its way to Europe. Palmistry, otherwise known as chiromancy, is the art of reading others through the study of the palm. It consists of reading the shape, various lines, and mounts (bumps) present on the hand in order to evaluate a person's character or future. Each of these aspects on the hand is read in relation to its various qualities and attributes, in order to compile an impression or reading of the person in question. As with most forms of divination and fortune telling there is no 'hard' set of rules - all palm readers will have different methods and preferences that work for them. Many will start by reading the dominant hand first, but there is no right or wrong way. As with everything else, the key to success is in experimenting over time and finding a method that works best for you.

Handshapes, finger length mounts, and minor lines can all be taken into consideration when reading palms. However, there are three major lines on the palm. The heart (love) line, the head (wisdom) line, and the life line. These are an excellent place to start when learning to read palms. The three main minor lines are known as the sun (Apollo line), the fate line, and the health line. By means of an introduction to this fascinating art, I have included detailed descriptions and interpretations of these six lines. Whilst there is, of course, far more on the palm that can be taken into account, these six lines will give you a solid introduction into the art of Chiromancy.

It is also worth noting that the aura of a person can also be picked up during palm readings which can provide you with further insight into the person whose hand you are studying. It is not necessary to read every single line on the palm. Listen to your intuition and pick out the lines that your gut feelings suggest are of the most importance.

THE HEART LINE

The heart line, also known as the love line, gives an indication about a person's emotional state of being and their emotional and physical relationships with others. It can also be considered to be a predictor of heart health. This heart line is located above the head line and life line. It starts either under the index finger or middle finger and extends toward the little finger. Many clues relating to love and relationships can be revealed by just the position of the line on the palm.

If the heart line begins underneath the index finger, it is an indication that you are satisfied with your love life, or it could mean that you are picky about who you choose to have a relationship with. If it begins underneath the middle finger, this can signify a self-centered approach to love, or that the person in question may be overly focused on the need to be loved. A line that starts between the middle and index fingers indicates that they are quick to give away their love. If the line crosses the fate line, it can indicate the possibility of a significant relationship loss. Below are some meanings and interpretations of the various shapes, depths, and lengths of the heart line:

A long heart line indicates a person who is open and has an overall warmth. It can also indicate having a naïve belief that there are perfect relationships. If the heart line is very long and touches both ends of the palm, it shows signs of co-dependency toward their partners or possible promiscuity. A short heart line is indicative of a highly self-centered individual.

A deep heart line indicates a stressful life. A deep and straight heart line is indicative of someone with a tendency towards feelings of jealousy, or someone who tends to have issues with authority.

A straight heart line demonstrates a more passive tendency in love relationships or can signal someone who is void of emotion and or whose emotions are ruled by the head over the heart.

A heart line that is straight and short indicates an individual who is not particularly concerned with romance. If the heart line is straight and parallel to the head line it demonstrates an emotionally stable individual. A heart line that has a wavy appearance represents a history of many love relationships, or a lack of serious relationships. If a heart line is curved it indicates a very physical and emotional, sensitive and intuitive individual. It can also represent somebody who expresses feelings easily.

A clear, deep heart is indicative of a person who is sincere, considerate and respectful, secure in themselves and at peace with their emotions. However, if the heart line is red and darker it represents a more temperamental approach to life, which can make them either very easy-going or quick to anger. A lighter red heart line represents a more removed, stoic, and cold emotional state.

A heart line that is faint represents a person who is aloof and places little importance on emotional life. A broken heart line indicates a person who is frequently emotionally stressed and can have a tendency towards mood swings or suffers from emotional trauma.

If the heart line is chained it demonstrates an individual who is easily hurt, has feelings of unhappiness, can have a tendency towards being indecisive, or can also represent a time of significant depression in their life.

A line that is double forked indicates that a person's life combines romance with practicality and common sense, whereas a triple forked heart line demonstrates that there is good balancing between your logical, physical, and emotional sides. If a heart line is absent it can indicate a level of ruthlessness or a person who is ruled by logic and may have a disregard for others. A heart line free from any branches indicates a lack of ability for emotional growth. If branches are present and move in an upwards direction this represents a person having a strong interest in the opposite sex and an ability to maintain healthy and positive relationships.

If branches point in a downwards direction it can represent an unhealthy or unhappy relationship.

THE LIFE LINE

The line on the palm that people are often the most curious about is the life line. This line begins between the index finger and the thumb and continues in a downwards direction towards the base of the thumb and the connection to the wrist. It is a common misconception that the life line can reveal how long you will live or when you will die. It does, however, reveal information about the encounters that you may have in your life, relationships with others, a person's health, and their physical and emotional well-being.

Listed below are some common interpretations of the various shapes, depths and lengths of the life line:

A long and deep life line indicates overall good health, stamina, vitality, and a well-balanced individual, whereas if the life line is short and deep it is a testament to the ability to overcome physical problems. It is a widely believed myth that a short life line signifies a short life. If the life line is short and shallow, it simply signifies that other people can easily influence or control a person. A deep life line suggests a smoother life path. If a life line is particularly faint this suggests a person with low energy and having a less adventurous life.

If a life line is broken this indicates struggles, losses, unexpected change, or interruption in your way of living, or perhaps an accident or illness. A break in the life line on one hand can signify that you may get ill and recover quickly whereas a break in the life line on both hands can signify that you may suffer a serious illness or disease. If there is a break near the wrist area in the line, it can indicate that problems occurred in early childhood.

A chained life line suggests that you are likely to be susceptible to health or emotional problems. A forked line has various meanings depending on the fork placement on the hand. Generally speaking, forks indicate an interruption or dramatic change in your life's purpose and direction. It can also sometimes indicate that you are surrounded by scattered, unbalanced, or split energies. A double or triple life line is usually seen in a person who is generally surrounded by positive energies and has good stamina. However, in some instances, this can suggest that a person may be living a double life. If the life line is absent this indicates a particularly highly-strung, anxious and nervous individual.

If a life line is branched, upward branches indicate achievement and success and downward branches indicate poor physical and emotional health, financial instability, feelings of sadness and loss. Lines extending up and above the life line show a good ability to recover from situations. Lines extending below the life line signify habitually wasting energy.

THE HEAD LINE

The head line, also known as the wisdom line, is considered to be one of the most important lines in Chinese palmistry, this line reveals a person's mental and psychological makeup, intellectual development and intuitive abilities. The head line begins just above the life line, between the thumb and the index finger and runs across the palm toward the other edge of the palm horizontally. Sometimes the head line begins directly on the life line and extends out from there. This indicates a person of strong will. Listed below are some further interpretations of the various lengths, shapes, and depths of the head line:

A long head line indicates high intelligence and a good memory. This is representative of a person who thinks things with care and logic and who does not overreact. They will take a calm and considered view of many possibilities before taking any final action. If a head line is so long that it extends across the entire width of the palm this indicates a highly successful individual, free from any cowardice, although those with this sort of head line may also demonstrate somewhat selfish tendencies.

A particularly straight head line indicates an individual who is realistic, practical, down-to-earth, materialistic, logical, good organizational skills or has exhibits good attention to detail. However, if the head line is long and straight it suggests a versatile, complex individual. A notably short head line indicates a practical and straight forward individual who does not beat around the bush.

A deep head line denotes an excellent memory, good concentration, and a sensible nature. If this line is wavy it can signify significant inner conflict within an individual's practical and emotional sides. It can also indicate an individual who is untrustworthy, restless, unstable or has a short attention span.

Curved or sloping head lines indicate a romantic, creative and idealistic individual who is open to new ideas and is who is seldom afraid to investigate new or alternative concepts or beliefs. This person usually has great trust in their intuition. A faint head line signifies an inability to concentrate or a lack of ability to demonstrate common sense. If a head line is broken this can demonstrate inconsistent thinking or tendencies towards nervousness and mental exhaustion. Crosses on the head line indicate the vital and crucial decisions made in one's life that can have a direct impact on your fate in your life.

A chained head line is demonstrative of an individual who is currently undergoing personal conflict, melancholy or confusion and who often has difficulty in setting positive goals.

If a head line is forked and the line ends with a strong fork, it is sometimes referred to as a writer's fork or lawyer's fork. A person with this variation of line usually enjoys debates and can clearly see both sides of an issue. It also indicates great imagination and someone who uses their psychic gifts, writing or speaking abilities successfully throughout their life. A hooked head line indicates a self-centered or untrustworthy individual. If the hook sits low on the palm, the individual is likely to be somewhat miserable, selfish, and cheap.

Branches occurring on the head line signify events that are yet to come to pass. They can also represent distractions that take an individual off their intellectual path. If branched in an upwards direction they show likely positive outcomes and success in career, academics, and creativity. When branches point in a downwards direction it signifies the occurrence of struggles, possible depression, sorrow, distress and disappointments at various points in that person's life.

An absent head line is an extremely rare occurrence; however, it can sometimes indicate laziness, sluggishness, dullness or even a marked detachment from reality.

The presence of a Double head line indicates increased brainpower. It can also represent a pleasant person, or in direct contrast to this a particularly cruel individual.

THE FATE LINE

The Fate line is widely considered to be one of the most important lines in palmistry. When searching for your own fate line look for the vertical line that travels from the palm area towards the base of the middle finger. For some people this line it begins at the base of the palm, whilst for others it starts nearer to the middle area of the palm.

A clear, solid, and straight Fate line free from too many marks or crosses indicates that you most likely have a reasonably good, peaceful, and fulfilling life.

The fate line also holds indications of timings. The timings on the fate line are usually read by imagining numbering on the fate line, starting from the base of the palm and indicates the various ages of the person concerned. The head line makes the point of approximately 35 years of age. This enables you to roughly gauge how a person's fate may pan out across different stages of their lives.

Absence of the fate line does not indicate bad luck or no career at all. All it implies is that you are always on the lookout for newer opportunities and are likely to be a person prone to frequently changing your job. This is suggestive of the fact that you have likely not yet found your ideal profession or are careless and find it difficult to stay focused on a particular task.

A long, deep, and straight fate line that travels right from the base of the palm to the Mount of Saturn (just below the middle finger) is found present on the palm of a person who has a strong sense of ability with regards to managing their career or business, and who also lays a heavy emphasis on creditability and dedication. A narrow fate line that becomes weaker from the middle part of the palm suggests a bright career start that has become less successful over time. A shallow fate line indicates hard work and perseverance despite being faced with numerous difficulties. If the line is shallow but wide, it means life's road is tough and a person may not necessarily accomplish great things.

The positioning of the fate line also carries some significance. If the fate line begins to join up with the life line, it demonstrates that you are a strong personality who is full of life and often bursting with energy, who is fairly satisfied and content with their life. If the fate line begins at the head line, it indicates the onset of success and achievements after reaching the age of 35. Before that age, you may feel that you are faced with countless roadblocks and problems that threaten to deter your growth. If the fate line starts from the heart line this also indicates success somewhat later in life. People faced with such scenarios are generally a little unstable when it comes to career related decisions during their youth. They often begin to see glimpses of success during the later years of their life and as a result will often be required to work hard into their old age. If the head line cuts the fate line off causing it to end it indicates that a person will likely discontinue work, perhaps due to a poor judgment or inappropriate decision. A break in the fate line from the base of the palm indicates the likelihood of a rough childhood and possible academic disruptions, whereas a break stemming from the middle of the palm indicates the likelihood setbacks and problems in a career or a loss of property in the later years of life.

When islands appear on the fate line, it indicates blocks on the career front. An island at the point where the fate line crosses the head line is suggestive of financial loss or a career tarnished by poor choices or decisions. An island at the point where the fate line joins the heart line indicates career related difficulties that are likely to have been affected by your emotions. If the fate line is chained at its beginning, it is demonstrative of a potentially unhappy and unsatisfied life that has likely prevented a person from concentrating on their studies during the early years of student life, resulting in poor examination marks. If the fate line is chained at its end this often indicates career problems during older age and other problems stemming from financial losses.

THE SUN LINE

The sun line or Apollo line is so named because of its positioning on the hand, starting its journey from the Mount of Moon (located on the base of the palm, on the side of the little finger) and descends upwards to the Mount of Sun which is located just below the ring finger. You may naturally presume that those blessed with a long sun line would be likely to be successful popular, and talented in comparison to those who may have a shorter sun line or those with no sun line at all. But it is not that straightforward. If you have a strong fate line but a weak sun line, no matter, how hard you may try, success and recognition will be likely to escape you. However, even if you have a reasonably moderate fate line but your sun line is particularly strong, you will likely find success.

A short or absent sun line indicates that a person enjoys a reasonable simple and ordinary life. Success, reputation or infamy are unlikely to be a part of their life. If the sun line is entirely absent, it is a constant uphill struggle to achieve success despite repeated attempts and failures. A shorter sun line indicates a person who is unlikely to enjoy success until the later years of life.

People blessed with a clear and very visible sun line are often avid art and literature fans. A narrow line indicates a possibly turbulent marriage and numerous other frustrations in life.

The positioning of the sun line also carries considerable importance. A sun line that begins at the base of the palm and ends near the center of the hand indicates the likelihood of great success at a young age that begins to spiral downwards as mid-life approaches. A primary reason for this is the onset of satisfaction that a person could begin to feel at this age which results in them discontinuing to put in the required additional effort in order to achieve further success.

A sun line that starts at the base of the palm and stops near the head line indicates good luck and fortune at a young age. If the sun line begins nearer the center of the hand, it often indicates a person who was slightly slower to blossom. The early life of such people has often been extremely difficult, but with persistence and dedication, they will start seeing success from mid-life onwards. If the sun line begins at the heart line and ends at the base of the ring finger it usually indicates a strong inclination towards arts. However, if the sun line starts from the fate line and moves towards the top, it is demonstrative of outstanding achievements and often suggests admiration from fellow acquaintances due to diligent hard work and effort.

If the sun line starts at the life line, it suggests that you are extraordinarily talented and enjoy an important academic position in life. These people are often great with words and can frequently be considered to be highly talented writers.

A sun line that begins at the Mount of Moon (located on the base of the palm on the side of the little finger) traveling up to the top, suggests fame and success. This person is likely to have achieved this success based on their associations and support from others. This line variation is frequently found in musicians, writers, and those connected to the entertainment industry. A broken sun line indicates frustration relating to a person's career. An intermittent sun line indicates the likelihood of constant interruption throughout life that can prove to be a hindrance to your success. A wavy sun line demonstrates a lack of confidence and someone who is often wary of accepting challenges. Success frequently eludes such people as they are challenged with numerous difficulties of life.

THE HEALTH LINE

It pretty much goes without saying that the health line in palmistry is associated with the health condition of a person. There is no fixed point at which it begins. It can begin from the base of the little finger and extend down across the palm to the base of the thumb, but it can also start under the heart line and end without joining with the life line. In Chinese palmistry, the line of health is also sometimes referred to as the unhealthy line. It usually appears in the hands of the person who is not of optimal health. But this does not mean that all kinds of health lines are bad. A straight line without touching the life line usually indicates a favorable health condition.

If you find your health line absent in your hand, this is a good sign. It means you are generally healthy and are unlikely to have any significant health problems.

A wavy line warns of potential health problems in the digestive system or a decline of liver or gallbladder function. There is a high chance for you to suffer from gastrointestinal disorder. If the health line bent into a big arc, it can indicate a significant loss of strength or vigor.

A broken line suggests a decline in the function of the digestive system. If your health line is crossed by some short lines, it indicates a poor health and you may tend to be prone to accidents. If the health line is particularly short or is composed of many shorter lines then this also indicates ill health, sickness or overall weakness.

Islands or donuts present on the health line indicate that you may suffer diseases of the liver, have a comparatively poor kidney function or experience issues relating to the respiratory system. If the island is large, it can sometimes be an indication of mammary gland hyperplasia disease for female. A chained health line is usually demonstrative of somebody having a poor health condition relating to compromised liver function.

The presence of a star on the health line indicates difficulty in obtaining support and help from family members. Women who have a star at the crossing point of head line and health line usually have a difficult delivery or suffer with issues relating to infertility. If the star forms a black area, it suggests that you may suffer serious mental disorder when following a birth. Men who have such a star usually have a low sexual function which can lead to difficulties regarding reproduction.

A cross beside the health line denotes an increased likelihood accidental bodily damages which will negatively impact on your health. If there is a triangle present on the health line it suggests that you are likely to have some problem in the area of mental health.

It is important to keep in mind that these indicators of overall health are in no way medically diagnostic. They are simply an indicator and usually nothing to be overly concerned or panicked about.

BEYOND THE VEIL

Spirit Before Ego

"Spirit before ego". Three simple little words that I heard from someone whose name I cannot remember. These words have stuck with me throughout my own spiritual journey and I want to share them with you all now. Not for any particular reason other than the fact that I personally feel it is an important notion to always keep close to your heart, and what better time to become acquainted with this concept than right now, at the very start of your journey into spiritual and psychic development.

I was given a particularly horrifying yet perfect example of this a few years ago, and at the time I shared it with those students who I was mentoring. I am going to share it now with you all, in the hope that it helps the mantra of 'spirit before ego' to stick with you too.

Some time ago, I was contacted by a member of my Facebook group, "The Psychic Hideaway". It was over a trivial matter pertaining to the general day to day running of the group, but once the issue at hand had been dealt with, this person randomly started telling me about two young girls, both in spirit that he claimed to be 'counseling'. He told me their names but living on the other side of the world to him I had absolutely no idea who they were and had never before heard their names. He quickly proceeded to explain to me that these two young girls had sadly been murdered and that there were supposedly thousands of psychic mediums throughout his country attempting to 'solve the case' by communicating with the spirits of these two girls. He was very keen to tell me how much he was 'helping them' by asking them continually for clues as to who the perpetrator was. He then told me very matter of factly that they would "be able to cross over" once they had helped him to solve the case. I immediately felt sick. Something didn't sit right at all and my intuition was screaming at me. Out of curiosity and guided by my intuition I typed their names into *Google*. In a matter of seconds my internet browser was flooded with images. The moment I saw their photos the spirits of these two young girls turned up in my home and I instantly burst into tears. They just wanted to cross over and were desperate for help in doing so. They were being contacted over and over again by SO many people, being asked to go over and over their trauma and show people exactly what had happened to them. All they really wanted was help to cross. Still in tears, I spoke to them for a while before assisting them in crossing over. Still quite overwhelmed with sadness I messaged the man I had been speaking with, believing fully in my naivety that he would be happy for them to have found peace. Having boasted to me at length about how he was counselling them and 'helping them', I was both shocked and horrified at his response.

"What? You crossed them over? Does this mean they won't be able to tell me anything anymore?"

That was his only concern. That his 'source' of information had been removed and he wouldn't get to 'crack the case'. He wouldn't get to be the hero or have his 15 minutes of fame. Never has there been a clearer example of ego being put before spirit.

I am sharing this story with you now because it's such a clear example of the ego getting in the way of helping those who are truly in need.

Ego is a word that is commonly thrown around in the spiritual community and considered to be somewhat 'dirty'. But the ego is also commonly misunderstood. So often it is confused for confidence and the two commonly become misinterpreted and intertwined leaving people frequently left wondering what the difference between ego and confidence actually is. Confidence is so important, and confidence is a great thing that we should all strive to achieve and also to protect. It is fragile and easily knocked and dented. We need confidence in ourselves in order to be able to trust in our gifts, our intuition and our own abilities. Ego is a very different little devil that we must try to leave at the door.

One of the big differences between ego and confidence is that we all have an ego. Not everyone has confidence. Each person's ego is different. Some people have terribly fragile egos whilst others have egos that have become so overly inflated that they can barely pass through an open doorway. Many people rely on the ego as a method of self-protection that they use to hide or disguise their own perceived weakness and vast insecurities. The ego is a projection of our false self, that allows people to show others an outward appearance of confidence that is usually not truly present.

We will all almost certainly have come across a person at some point in our lives who is particularly good at something, often considerably better than their peers in that one specific area, who feels compelled to make damn sure that everybody is aware of their superiority. Ego tells that person that in making it clear how much better than everyone else they are in this one particular area, then they may well be led to believe that they are superior to them in every way. This is the defense mechanism at work. In leading others to believe that they are superior to them in all walks of life, rather than pertaining only to their one particular skill or talent, they strive to hide the truth relating to their hidden weaknesses and insecurities. That projection of superiority is quite likely covering up for a whole multitude of insecurities in other areas. Ego attempts to steal the focus away from those insecurities and weaknesses by drawing attention to the one thing area that person is genuinely gifted in.

Ego tends to cause people to reject the opinions of others. This is clearly counterproductive to personal development and growth. Ego closes minds and obstructs vision so that people can no longer see anything other than their own ideas. Deepak Chopra, a well-known spiritual leader, once wrote "The ego relies on the familiar. It is reluctant to experience the unknown, which is the very essence of life." This statement suggests that ego will rarely allow people to stray from their comfort zones. Again, this is the protection mechanism at work. If a person steps out of their comfort zone they may discover, and more importantly, others may also discover that they actually do not truly excel at everything they turn their hands to. They may even be terrible at some things. We all have strengths and weaknesses, and to step out of one's comfort zone is to risk exposing the truth that we may in truth be only 'average' at something. The ego is an unhealthy attachment to us that we allow to govern us and take over because we become so deeply attached to our own ideas. We resent any thought of allowing our idea to be proven in any way inferior to that of anybody else. Because of this resentment, negative emotions are often displayed whilst facing any opinions that oppose our own. The ego will cause people to argue, become angry, and often try to bully or intimidate others in order to make our idea stand out as the strongest or the best.

People become so attached to their ideas that they simply cannot allow them to be considered as second best in comparison to anybody else's opinion. Those who have fallen victim to the ego will also frequently belittle, mock or attempt to cut others down, in order to make themselves look and feel superior by destroying others and attempting to make them appear inferior. They will tear others down to make themselves look and feel like the 'top dog'. Those displaying confidence as opposed to ego do not suffer from this issue. People with confidence will willingly and joyfully support others and raise them up at every given opportunity.

People with confidence in themselves will usually display tendencies towards being more reserved, more humble, and are actually open to the ideas and opinions of others. People with confidence allow their work or their actions speak for themselves and are free from the constant need to prove their superiority to others. They have no need to outwardly try to convince others that their way is better. People with confidence are not afraid to step out of their comfort zone, because their confidence assures them that they have the capability to adequately perform any task or duty placed before them. People with confidence know that they will be alright despite any opposition they may be faced with because they are not hiding behind a facade of false superiority.

With confidence comes self-respect and an ability trust in and respect our own opinions whilst feeling secure enough to extend respect and value to the opinions and views of others too. We are confident that we can allow the opposing opinion to be heard without feeling the threat of 'losing face'. However, when ego takes over, we become insecure and scared, fearful of exposing our own flaws and weaknesses. The fear of the opinions of others can quickly take over. Ego leads us to arguments, anger and ultimately to pain and hurt. However, confidence leads us to stability and peace.

In order to release the ego and begin to nurture self-confidence, we must first remember that our thoughts, feelings, and actions are all reflections of our inner-selves. If we notice ourselves being egotistical, we need to look within ourselves and evaluate our true feelings. If we discover that we are trying to mask our hidden insecurities, we must attempt to take steps to strengthen our confidence in this area. We must let go of our attachment to our own opinion. This is not to say that we have to stop having respect for our own opinions, but that we must strive to open our minds to the possibilities of the opinions of others. We open ourselves up to discovering the strength and courage required to step outside of our comfort zones. When we achieve this, we are subsequently able to transcend our ego and unveil a newly found confidence in ourselves. It is when we step outside of our comfort zones that the magic happens.

We must also be mindful of the fact that no matter what the depth of our abilities in any area, an overly inflated ego that demonstrates arrogance breeds nothing more than disrespect and loathing. When living in ego we will attract lower vibrations and as we have already discussed, like attracts like, so this will practically guarantee you attracting further negative energies and vibrations into your life. Disrespect also attracts enemies who will be more than a little keen to prove to others that you are really not as good as you believe yourself to be. Disrespect will also frequently attract drama. If you have true confidence in your abilities, you will feel no need to announce it to the whole world. If you are truly as good as you think you are then the world will see it on their own. They will believe and trust in your credibility, worth, and ability because your self-confidence will bring them peace and assurance. Confidence vibrates on a much higher frequency than ego. It will attract like-minded people and those who seek to reach a similar vibration themselves. This is something truly worthy of admiration and goal that we should all be striving to attain throughout our journey.

Common Stumbling Blocks

Spiritual development and the psychic arts are not something that can be mastered overnight. As in all walks of life, as we evolve in any area, we will face a continuous and ever fluid journey of growth, periods of apparent stagnation, frustrations, joy, wonderment, and sometimes disbelief. If we choose this path and aspire to follow it from a place of love, a quest for personal growth and with confidence rather than ego, we can continue to evolve on a spiritual and psychic level throughout our entire lifetime.

As with most things, growth will often come in ebbs and flows and allowing this development to occur at its own natural pace, without chasing or trying to force things is optimal. However, there are some particularly common stumbling blocks that I am frequently approached about, and I hope that it will prove useful to address some of the most recurrently asked questions here.

"My guides are trying to show me something and I'm just not getting it. I had 'such and such' dream, then 'this' happened in a vision. 'So and so' said this, then someone else said this, and then that other reader said that, and I just can't seem to understand the message. What are they trying to tell me? Why aren't I getting it?"

Okay, so admittedly this is somewhat of a vaguely worded example, but I'm sure that you get the gist of the confusion and anxiety that usually accompanies this type of question. My answer to this question is almost always the same. "Let it go! Stop driving yourself crazy trying to fit together a multitude of mismatched pieces. This will only lead to immense frustration which will almost certainly create blockages and lower your vibrations. This is entirely counterproductive." If something is truly of importance, then eventually your guides will hit you around the head with it so forcefully and clearly that you simply will not be able to mistake the message. Not all jigsaw pieces can be forced together to create a single perfect image so don't waste your valuable time and energy trying to force things to fit into a logical and pretty little picture. Let it go, put it to one side, and if it's truly important your guides and the universe will ensure that you get the message when you actually need it.

Overthinking can without a doubt be one of our biggest pitfalls. Once we become aware of just how much spirit and the universe actually impacts on our lives, it can be easy to fall into the trap of trying constantly to interpret the 'meaning' of every single little thing that happens as we go about our day. Not everything is a sign or a message, and if we can manage to stop obsessing over finding an explanation for everything, then we become more easily able to actually relax and hear the true messages that we are being sent. We also open up our ability to recognize these messages for what they truly are.

Overthinking is such a common problem for so many of us. In tackling this issue, journaling can be of enormous benefit. I actually have a couple of students that I mentor who now frequently write in a 'journal of f**kery'. In the past, these students would wake up each morning and spend hour upon hour driving themselves crazy. They would analyze their dreams, trying desperately to match up random occurrences throughout their day with possible 'signs' or 'messages', in an attempt to just 'make sense of it all'. This can become a huge spiritual blockage born from frustration and the resulting lowered vibrations. So I advised them to start a 'journal of f**kery'. I suggested that each morning when they woke up, they documented their dream experiences in this journal, before putting it away somewhere out of sight. When these thoughts are taken out of your head and put onto paper it allows you to stop thinking and obsessing over it, safe in the knowledge that you no longer need to remember every tiny little detail. Should it ever become relevant in the future, you can easily access the information that you need. This allows you the freedom to let go of the baggage that is distracting you from being present in the now. For this reason, journaling of any description can be a wonderful tool for supporting development. Not only does it allow you to 'let stuff go, but it also means that should you ever feel it necessary to remind yourself of a past occurrence, then you are able to easily access the information which you seek.

"I am just no good at this - I feel like I'm just not as good as everyone else"

We all have areas of weakness……. And we each have areas of strength. We are all different, and that is what makes us beautiful. It genuinely does not matter if you are weak in one particular area of gifts or readings because you will almost certainly have other areas in which you excel. It may take a while to find your areas of strength, but you will find them eventually. Whilst you are doing so, those others who you are comparing yourself to now will perhaps be discovering their own areas of weakness. Focus on discovering your strengths rather than dwelling on your weaknesses.

Do not compare yourself to others. Each of us is unique, and even those of us with similar gifts will still have varying strengths, skills, and methods of doing things. Spiritual and psychic development is not a competition, and when we compare ourselves to others, we do nothing but devalue our own worth and damage our own self-confidence.

"I'm rubbish at visualization so guided meditations and shielding don't work for me"

So often, people are under the misguided impression that visualization automatically involves seeing a physical manifestation of an image or object.

This is simply not necessary. I am a clairvoyant, have frequent visions, and see spirit clearly with the naked eye. I am also an artist and a highly visual person, and I can't always visualize in that way either! It is simply of no importance. Yes, some people are highly skilled at visualization, but we all have different strengths, weaknesses, and abilities, and it just doesn't matter in the grand scheme of things. You can visualize in your mind's eye, and if necessary, even just focus on trying to imagine the image in your head. It will still have the desired effect. Remember that intention is what really matters. Trust in the process. The better you are able to stop chasing the results, the more you allow yourself to relax and open up your energy and senses. This often results in the process becoming easier and more comfortable over time.

"I did a reading and the person that I read for was not happy. They said my reading was no good and didn't resonate with them at all."

Trust yourself. Having a difficult sitter or querent can be incredibly taxing and can damage your confidence enormously. However, there are numerous points to take into consideration. Just because the person you read for said that your reading didn't resonate, this doesn't necessarily mean there was anything 'wrong' with your reading at all. We are all human, and we all have off days, this is very true, but more often than not there are other reasons why a reading may not be taken well.

When we read, we are passing on messages from spirit. Sometimes a person will ask for a reading without actually being prepared to listen to what spirit has to tell them. Sometimes they will not be ready to hear the truth, and it is not unheard of for people to jump from one online psychic reading group to another, asking the same questions repeatedly and not accepting a single reading until someone comes along and tells them what they want to hear. At other times a person may tell you following their reading that it doesn't not resonate with them at all. Often this person will then come back to you a few weeks later and inform you that in the days following their reading, a situation arose unexpectedly, leaving everything that you had told them suddenly making perfect sense. When people first delve into online reading groups, they will often spend a considerable amount of time providing free readings for strangers as they develop in confidence and ability. Unfortunately, it is not uncommon for psychic readers to experience extreme ingratitude at times in these groups. When somebody has spent so much of their time and energy providing a reading, I am often quite infuriated to discover that they haven't received so much as a "thank you" for sharing their gifts. If you experience this, please do not allow it to dishearten you. Even more importantly, do not sit there convincing yourself that their lack of gratitude is a reflection of your reading. People can sadly be very rude and ungrateful at times, especially in free reading groups where they can mistakenly feel entitled to your time and energy. These things happen to the best of readers, and unfortunately you are almost certain to find yourself in this sort of position at some point in your journey. The best advice I could give you regarding this situation is to try not to take it personally. You almost certainly will take it personally on at least some level...... we all do, but trust in yourself, remain polite, courteous, and professional, wish them well and move on. Ground, shield, cleanse yourself, and try to forget about it. It happens. Chalk it up to experience and if you managed not to cry then give yourself an extra pat on the back (because the truth is that we have probably all cried about something like this during the beginning stages of our journey!).

"My sister in law/friend/random acquaintance keeps asking me to read for them all the time and it makes me feel uncomfortable"

Say no! You are not a performing monkey. Readings take a huge amount of time and energy and you are entitled to say no. Setting boundaries is hugely important. Without them, even with the best of intentions, people can and will take advantage of you. If we fail to set boundaries, then we are setting ourselves up for failure because we are not being mindful of our own needs. You are not obligated to read for anyone if you do not wish to do so. Even if a person contacts you for a paid reading and something feels off, you have every right to decline to take that booking. Our gifts deserve respect, both from ourselves and from others, and if you feel uncomfortable about reading for any person in any given situation then you have the right to say no. This applies whether the person in question is a friend, family member or a stranger. You must protect your own energy and sometimes that means setting hard boundaries and sticking to them.

Setting boundaries can prove to be a make or break area for many. Especially when we read a lot online, with differing time zones and the fact that we are almost instantly contactable and accessible. We have to learn to say no. I will freely admit that it took me years to grasp this concept. 85% of my clients are on the other side of the world. When they sit down for the evening and hop online it is midnight here in the UK. Yet for years I struggled to say no, or to tell people that they would have to wait until tomorrow, and I would allow myself to feel pressured to help them immediately. I would frequently still be awake at 3am or 4am in the morning, providing free help to people online. At times I barely even got so much as a thank you for my time and energy. I was absolutely exhausted on a permanent basis, but I still couldn't say no, because I wanted to help those who needed it. Eventually, it began to affect my health and I was forced to take time out. During this period of rest, my guides drew my attention to a random quote - "Your emergency is not my priority", and this is something I still get reminded of by my guides when my boundaries begin to weaken. No matter how much we want to help others we cannot continue to do so at the expense of our own health and energy. The saying that *"you can't pour from an empty cup"* really rings true here, and failure to set healthy boundaries and to subsequently stick to them, will eventually leave you unable to be of use to anyone at all.

I cannot avoid also touching on the concept of balance here too. Balance is critical. I so often see people (and admittedly I was once one of them) who suddenly find themselves opening up spiritually and it can feel like you have finally found that elusive 'missing link' that you have spent your entire life searching for. It can often feel as though the blinkers have suddenly been removed and all that 'real life stuff' falls into a newfound perspective. We often throw ourselves down our newly discovered path with such enormous enthusiasm that we can fail to see that we are beginning to neglect everything outside of this new world of discovery. This is especially easy to do given the technological wonderland in which we currently exist. We can't simply walk away from our reading room, office or computer screen and switch off. With smartphones and Facebook apps constantly within our reach, it can be incredibly difficult to switch off and take time out of cyberspace. I am still guilty of this to a certain extent. The first thing I do most mornings before I even roll out of bed is to respond to client enquiries on my phone, and I am frequently up late at night working once everyone else has gone to bed. Taking time out is critical to our spiritual, emotional, and mental wellbeing. In all the excitement of new discoveries and tangible growth we must always be mindful of maintaining our health and sanity by ensuring that we allow ourselves to switch off and relax at frequent intervals.

Lastly, but perhaps most importantly, find your tribe. Throughout your journey and spiritual awakening, you will meet many people. Some of these will come and go, and you will undoubtedly learn something from each and every one of them along the way, but eventually, I hope that you are blessed enough to find your tribe. The group of people who will support you and rejoice in your accomplishments as if they were their own, raise you up and allow you to do the same in return for them. We all have different gifts, and when we come together and work as a team in love and support of each other, encouraging each other to grow and strive for greatness, beautiful things happen, and we become stronger than any individual could ever hope to be. Life as a practicing psychic or medium can be pretty tough. Reading for others is often incredibly draining physically, mentally, and emotionally. People will often seek guidance from spirit during times of extreme turmoil and we must always ensure that our own energy, and sanity for that matter, is protected from these negative emotions. Taking steps to ensure that you are energetically protected from negativity is crucial of course, but never underestimate the importance of finding like-minded people who are able to support you, inspire you, raise you up when you are struggling to do it for yourself, who understand you and with whom you can bounce ideas around. They say that *'teamwork makes the dream work'*, and never has a saying been more appropriate. Often ego, competition, and envy, especially when working online, can threaten to tarnish the beauty presented to us by the exciting possibilities of our journey. Surround yourself with people who give as freely as they take, and who want your success as much as they want their own. These are the people who will dust your spiritual journey with magic.

"Sweet dreams, and may the dead let you rest."

"Real isn't how you are made," said the Skin Horse. "It's a thing that happens to you. When a child loves you for a long, long time, not just to play with, but REALLY loves you, then you become Real."

"Does it hurt?" asked the Rabbit.

"Sometimes," said the Skin Horse, for he was always truthful. "When you are Real you don't mind being hurt."

"Does it happen all at once, like being wound up," he asked, "or bit by bit?"

"It doesn't happen all at once," said the Skin Horse. "You become. It takes a long time. That's why it doesn't happen easily to people who break easily, or have sharp edges, or who have to be carefully kept. Generally, by the time you are Real, most of your hair has been loved off, and your eyes drop out and you get loose in the joints and very shabby. But these things don't matter at all, because once you are Real you can't be ugly, except to people who don't understand."

"The Velveteen Rabbit"
By Margery Williams

Useful Resources

Contact the author:
lucybaker.beyondtheveil@yahoo.com

Website:
www.lucy-baker.com

Liberatus School of Psychic Arts:
www.liberatuspsychicarts.com

The Psychic Hideaway Facebook Group:
https://m.facebook.com/groups/2050953568464375

Out of the Void:
For meticulously crafted dragons blood essence I cannot recommend Melanie at 'Out of the Void' highly enough. Melanie also handcrafts absolutely beautiful custom jewelry, and pendulum designs based on customers specified requirements.

https://www.facebook.com/melanieoutofthevoid

Haven:
Stacy's exquisitely handcrafted products are all created from 100% natural ingredients, focusing on healing, protecting the mind, body, soul, and raising your vibrations.

http://www.facebook.com/havenheals